Arjan Plaisier, Leo J. Koffeman (Eds.)

The Protestant Church in the Netherlands: Church Unity in the 21st Century

Church Polity and Ecumenism

Global Perspectives

edited by

Allan J. Janssen, Leo J. Koffeman,
Christina Landman, Johannes Smit
and C. Leon van den Broeke

Volume 4
(Special Edition)

LIT

The Protestant Church in the Netherlands: Church Unity in the 21st Century

Stories and Reflections

edited by

Arjan Plaisier and Leo J. Koffeman

LIT

Cover image: Dutchlight

This publication is sponsored by: La Fondation Pour l'Aide
au Protestantisme Réformé (Geneva)

This book is printed on acid-free paper.

Bibliographic information published by the Deutsche Nationalbibliothek
The Deutsche Nationalbibliothek lists this publication in the Deutsche
Nationalbibliografie; detailed bibliographic data are available in the Internet at
http://dnb.d-nb.de.

ISBN 978-3-643-90530-7

A catalogue record for this book is available from the British Library

©LIT VERLAG GmbH & Co. KG Wien,   LIT VERLAG Dr. W. Hopf
Zweigniederlassung Zürich 2014   Berlin 2014
Klosbachstr. 107   Fresnostr. 2
CH-8032 Zürich   D-48159 Münster
Tel. +41 (0) 44-251 75 05   Tel. +49 (0) 2 51-62 03 20
Fax +41 (0) 44-251 75 06   Fax +49 (0) 2 51-23 19 72
E-Mail: zuerich@lit-verlag.ch   E-Mail: lit@lit-verlag.de
http://www.lit-verlag.ch   http://www.lit-verlag.de

Distribution:

In the UK: Global Book Marketing, e-mail: mo@centralbooks.com
In North America: International Specialized Book Services, e-mail: orders@isbs.com
In Germany: LIT Verlag Fresnostr. 2, D-48159 Münster
Tel. +49 (0) 2 51-620 32 22, Fax +49 (0) 2 51-922 60 99, E-mail: vertrieb@lit-verlag.de

In Austria: Medienlogistik Pichler-ÖBZ, e-mail: mlo@medien-logistik.at
e-books are available at www.litwebshop.de

Table of contents

Reflections

Preface

Karin van den Broeke

The year 2014 marks the tenth anniversary of the Protestant Church in the Netherlands. Since May 1, 2004, the Netherlands Reformed Church, the Reformed Churches in the Netherlands, and the Evangelical Lutheran Church in the Kingdom of the Netherlands have been united in a single denomination known as the Protestant Church in the Netherlands. This jubilee of a young church with ancient legacies invites us to look back – and to glance ahead!

I remember December 12, 2003 like it was yesterday. The process in which the three churches had been involved for years and which – from my perspective – was so closely linked to Jesus' appeal for unity was completed. The synods of all three denominations made the decision to unite. Many people were extremely grateful that the three churches had found a way to give up part of their individuality for the sake of a deeper connection. Local congregations that had been living "Together on the Way" for decades were given an opportunity to enter into full unity. Men and women who had devoted themselves to the cause of bringing the churches together for years saw their dream come true. At the same time, it was clear that a new rift was bound to happen. Will visible unity in Christ ever be a simple matter?

In the meantime, ten years have passed. The Protestant Church in the Netherlands has shown itself to be a church that is able to combine its confessing character with room for diversity. Sharing faith is possible – and is a reality – in this church. Spiritual life, a tradition of living together, a commitment to serving the world, and a vigilant way of respecting creation are considered to be aspects of lifelong discipleship. In a world characterized by a rich variety of religions and beliefs, the Protestant Church in the

Netherlands points to the power that biblical sources have to serve as a life-giving Word.

It certainly is not always easy to be a church in the Netherlands in the twenty-first-century. Plurality and individualization represent challenges that require a careful balance of tradition and renewal on the part of the church. Sometimes the pain of losing what was well known is more intense than the delight of renewal. Nevertheless, that pain does not affect the power that exists in a united church.

In trying again and again, our united church represents a measure of reconciliation. Two confessional traditions have come together, one of which is numerically much stronger than the other. We try to do justice to both of them. As a united church, we know that we are accountable to the broader ecumenical movement. This unification is only part of the unity for which Christ prayed and to which he calls us. In the end, we yearn for a creation that is one and lives in peace, reconciled by Christ's love and guided by the transforming power of the Spirit.

I trust that in the years ahead, the Protestant Church in the Netherlands will continually be aware of its calling to witness to the power of reconciliation and to contribute to unity.

Rev. Karin van den Broeke
Moderator of the General Synod of the Protestant Church in the Netherlands

Introduction

Arjan Plaisier, Leo J. Koffeman

"We unite believing that our Lord Jesus Christ himself prayed for the unity of his Church, so that the world may believe in Him." These words from the Declaration on Unification, which was signed on Friday, December 12, 2005 in Utrecht, clearly express some of the deepest motivations for church unification. It was on this foundation that the Protestant Church in the Netherlands came into being on May 1, 2004, as the result of a merger between the Netherlands Reformed Church, the Reformed Churches in the Netherlands, and the Evangelical Lutheran Church in the Kingdom of the Netherlands.

This volume marks the tenth anniversary of the Protestant Church in the Netherlands (PCN). LIT-Verlag (Zürich) welcomed this venture and granted the book a place in a series entitled Church Polity and Ecumenism: Global Perspectives. The Fondation Pour L'aide Au Protestantisme Réformé in Geneva generously contributed a grant to this project. Joyce Mauler (Prague) provided an (American) English language check, and did so thoroughly.

This publication has a threefold purpose. Firstly, it is written "for the record," that is, to inform an international audience about the long history that preceded the unification and the developments that occurred during the first decade following 2004. To some extent, the contributions of Leo J. Koffeman, Arjan Plaisier, and Harm Dane in Part I have a documentary character; nevertheless, they also identify a number of issues that continue to challenge the PCN and, for that matter, other united and uniting churches.

That is why, secondly, we have also invited four authors from other countries to contribute to this volume by sharing the story of their church with us and by attempting to make some comparisons between that story and the PCN narrative. Hugh Robert Boudin (Belgium), Andrew Dutney

(Australia) Nico Koopmans (South Africa), and David M. Thompson (the United Kingdom) graciously accepted the invitation. Their contributions in Part II describe a range of different experiences, and taken together, they greatly enrich the picture of what church unification may entail and the kind of message that it may give. In fact, all of them – unlike the PCN story up to this point – tell a story of consecutive unions. It seems that once churches have united, they not only experience a certain impetus to pursue additional mergers; they may also be more skilled at executing such steps. Unification processes are learning processes, and what has been learnt can be put into practice again. This fact may demonstrate the relevance that this publication may have for the broader ecumenical movement.

Thirdly, this volume is also meant to contribute to ecumenical theology. That is why we have asked three theologians from different backgrounds to read the draft texts of Parts I and II and to share some reflections on theological issues that these articles may raise. Roman Catholic theologian and prominent member of the WCC Faith and Order Commission William Henn (USA, now Rome), Orthodox theologian and World Council of Churches staff member Daniel Buda (Rumania, now Geneva), and North American theologian Randi Walker were so kind as to respond positively to the invitation to complete the picture of practical experiences and living expectations.

As most of these stories show, church unifications tend to be the result of lengthy processes. The first steps toward the birth of the PCN were taken half a century ago. Many different factors play a role in such processes. Doctrinal and theological controversies may seem to be prominent, but in most cases, cultural aspects also make unification a complex matter. This is obvious, for instance, in post-apartheid South Africa, where ethnic and linguistic differences had (and still have) to be dealt with through a process of reconciliation. Yet, in a more hidden way, culture issues determine the pace of unification processes in other stories as well. Uniting churches may not have a comparable ethos because the way people deal with church life is shaped by historical experiences that are decisive for the manner in which they understand themselves. Characteristics that may seem to be quite irrelevant from the perspective of an outsider may be pivotal for ecclesial identity as that is perceived by insiders. Issues like the degree of autonomy that is accorded to local congregations or liturgical traditions can cause major delays if "the way we should do it" is seen as being equal to "the way we have always done it."

In some of the cases described in this volume, the unification was, in fact, a reunion: churches that had split long before found their way to renewed unity. This is particularly true of the Reformed partners in the Dutch context, where a nineteenth-century division had to be overcome. However, it did not make sense to try to "solve" the "original problem;" in the course of a century, both of the churches in question had developed separate identities with respect to issues that had not played a role at the time of the separation. Yet, in most cases described in this volume, the churches that united had not been one body previously. As far as the PCN is concerned, bringing together churches from the Reformed and the Lutheran traditions was a completely new enterprise.

Unification takes time – and usually even requires a lot of time. It may sometimes seem as if churches can virtually split overnight (although a long history of increasing tension may precede the actual separation). However, healing conflict – or even getting to know each other – is usually a time-consuming matter. Mutual trust has to grow, but if that really happens and results in church unification, it can be experienced as a miracle of the Holy Spirit.

Two of the churches that share their stories in this volume – the Uniting Church in Australia and the Uniting Reformed Church in Southern Africa – explicitly chose to include the adjective "uniting" in their names. Not only does this decision reveal these churches' readiness to take further steps involving other churches on the path of unification. It also points to an important characteristic of unification processes: they are never really completed. Unification is an ongoing process even after the formal act of unification like the one that occurred on May 1, 2004 in the case of the PCN. National and local levels may need to proceed at a different pace. Organizational unity does not necessarily entail full spiritual unity. New issues – be they theological, ethical, or cultural in nature – require further processes of fostering mutual trust, finding agreement, and making decisions. Changing contexts produce challenges that were unknown before. There is always a risk that satisfaction with the unity that has been achieved will lead to complacency and that new challenges will not be taken up. Unity can be eroded and, in fact, may mask a (growing) lack of identity in the areas of theology and ethics – which may finally make the mission of the church ineffective. Therefore, it is important to recognize the role that a reconsideration and renewal of their mission agendas plays in the life of the churches that are presented in this volume. The "unity we seek" – to use a well-known ecumenical expression – is not just a matter of finding a shared structure; above all, it is a matter of sharing in a common mission. Unity without a shared mission is pointless, mission without unity is ambiguous.

Those who are familiar with the outcome of recent consultations regarding united and uniting churches that have been sponsored by the Faith and Order Commission of the World Council of Churches will easily recognize that unity and mission usually go hand in hand. This is also a pivotal insight of the most recent report of the Faith and Order Commission on ecclesiology, which is entitled *The Church: Towards a Common Vision* (CTCV). A pertinent passage reads:

In the Church, through the Holy Spirit believers are united with Jesus Christ and thereby share a living relationship with the Father, who speaks to them and calls forth their trustful response. The biblical notion of *koinonia* has become central in the ecumenical quest for a common understanding of the life and unity of the Church. This quest presupposes that communion is not simply the union of existing churches in their current form. … As a divinely established communion, the Church belongs to God and does not exist for itself. It is by its very nature missionary, called and sent to witness in its own life to that communion God intends for all humanity and for all creation in the kingdom (CTCV, § 13).

The stories and reflections presented in this volume cannot help but raise questions regarding what the future may hold for united and uniting churches. The vast majority of the denominations belonging to this category of churches are made up of Protestant churches, and particularly of those with deep historical roots. Churches belonging to the Catholic or Orthodox traditions and – on the other side of the spectrum – Pentecostal or Evangelical churches are scarcely involved in unification processes. The latter do not participate in such processes because they are almost entirely focused on local faith communities, while the former tend to be either national or international churches and therefore, can hardly unite with other churches without giving up vital historical claims. Anglican churches, however, have often taken the lead in unification processes. Protestants like Methodists, Lutherans, and Reformed denominations (that include Presbyterians and Congregationalists) are better able – and more willing – to meet the challenge, although this does not necessarily make them forerunners in the necessary renewal of church life in the twenty-first century. One the one hand, their readiness to seek unity attests to their strength – as many of the stories in this volume suggest. They feel called to take this avenue, and they demonstrate a capability to do this from a mission perspective because they are aware of the opportunities and threats of this time. The choice to unite is in itself a choice to pursue renewal and a sign of transformation. Differences that have been able to keep such churches separated for decades or even centuries seem to be outdated. On the other hand, these denominations can become focused on simply maintaining existing structures and practices as easily as any other church. Nevertheless, at the very least, church unification will always imply a challenge to renew church life. That is what the PCN has experienced again and again.

Only the future will reveal what the value of this renewal is. All we can do is accept our responsibility, praying "Come, Holy Spirit, renew your Church!"

Abbreviations and bibliography

CTCV: The Church – Towards a Common Vision. Faith and Order Paper 214. Geneva: WCC Publications 2013.

PCN: Protestant Church in the Netherlands.

WCC: World Council of Churches.

Part I

The Story of the Protestant Church in the Netherlands

How the Protestant Church in the Netherlands was born

Leo J. Koffeman

Introduction

The Protestant Church in the Netherlands (PCN) was born on May 1, 2004, as the result of a merger of three churches. Two churches, which both belonged to the Reformed tradition, were reunited. They were the two major Reformed denominations of the Calvinist tradition in the Netherlands: the Netherlands Reformed Church (NRC) and the Reformed Churches in the Netherlands (RCN). The NRC included a number of French-speaking, 'Walloon' congregations. Two consecutive splits within the NRC in 1834 and 1886 initially resulted in two separate church communities. Those groups united in 1892 to form the RCN. The unification process in 2004 also included the Evangelical Lutheran Church in the Kingdom of the Netherlands (ELC), a small church in terms of membership, which nevertheless represented an internationally important branch of Protestantism.

Some statistical data may provide a sense of the significance of this process. In 2004, about 16 million inhabitants were living in the Netherlands. At that time, the NRC had about 1,300 local congregations, numbering some 1,900,000 members. Among those were about 400,000 "other members," i.e. non-baptized people who were included on the roll because their parents had belonged to the NRC. The RCN only included baptized members in its statistics. At the time, it had about 660,000 members in 850 local congregations. Lastly, with about 15,000 members in some 60 congregations, the Lutheran partner church was among the smallest denominations in the Netherlands. The number of ministers active in the congregations was around 1,450; 890; and 30, respectively. Overall, about 1 percent of the members of the new PCN represented the Lutheran tradition.

The history of the unification can be divided into two main phases. It took about twenty-five years to cultivate the degree of theological consensus (and mutual spiritual trust) that made it possible to decide in favor of some form of unification. In the second phase, preparations had to be made regarding church polity and organization; these finally resulted in the birth of the PCN. In this article I will first describe these two phases before making a few evaluative remarks in a concluding section.

1 Towards theological consensus as a basis for unification (1962–1990)

1.1 Exploring

The merger of the NRC, RCN, and ELC into the PCN took place as the result of a process that extended over four decades. During the first phase, which began in 1962, everything was still completely open. The only clear thing was that the churches' (lack of) credibility necessitated new thoughts about the relationship between the NRC and the RCN. In fact, the unification process grew of a mission perspective. It was launched in 1962 at the initiative of eighteen ministers from the NRC and the RCN who were working in mission settings (e.g. as student pastors). They expressed the conviction that by continuing their separate existences, the churches had seriously hampered the credibility of the gospel and the churches' power to witness to Jesus Christ. A few years later, the youth organizations of both churches revitalized this process.

1.2 Meeting

The second phase of the reunification process began in 1973 with the first joint session of the general synods of the NRC and the RCN and continued at a second session in 1976. Now, the first more official type of connection could start to take shape. Around the same time, both churches – along with the ELC – adopted the *Leuenberg Agreement* (LA). In this document, Lutheran, Reformed, and United churches as well as some pre-Reformation churches, from all over Europe, formally declared that the mutual condemnations of the Reformation era were no longer valid, due to the common understanding of the gospel that was formulated in the LA. However, at this stage of the process in the Netherlands, there was no reference to the LA's possible significance for the two churches' relationship with one another.

The unification process was, first and foremost, a grass-roots movement. That is where its power has manifested itself over the decades. Beginning in 1979, what was known as the "Interim Order" was gradually developed: special church laws were written for local situations where two or more congregations wanted to work together intensively (that is, as if they were, in fact, one congregation). After such congregations had entered into a "federation agreement", the rules of the separate churches with regard to a number of issues no longer needed to be followed, if the Interim Order had made arrangements in that respect. Later (beginning in 1982), such laws were also applied to the churches' regional assemblies. However, it was clear that what was stipulated in these laws was in no way meant to be determinative of – or decisive for – the final form of the future united church.

By 2004, the number of formally approved federation agreements had risen above 400 on the local level, but even this number was not a good gauge of the extent to which congregations were "together on the way" (as the unification process was usually known). Many congregations worked together without formalizing this cooperation in a federation agreement. By the same year, out of seventy-five "classes" (presbyteries or regional assemblies) in the NRC and the RCN, twenty-eight had already opted for federation, and another twenty-two were cooperating closely. Six of the nine provincial assemblies (a higher regional level) were also federated.

1.3 Deciding

Between 1973 and 1986, the General Synods of the NRC and the RCN were primarily concerned with the question of whether there were theological and ecclesiological factors that would make further union impossible. In 1986, those considerations led a "combi-synod" (a joint meeting of the two synods) to adopt a Declaration of Intent and a Declaration of Consensus. The conclusion was quite clear: there were no theological reasons for continuing to go our separate ways. Shortly after that, the ELC joined the discussion; thus, the process of reuniting also became a process of unification, with three churches from two different confessional traditions participating.

Ecclesiological points of reference regarding the formation of the PCN can mainly be found in the documents mentioned above – that is, in the Declaration of Intent and the Declaration of Consensus – and in the Lutheran response to these documents, which confirmed the ELC's entry into the process. The Declaration of Intent is quite short. In it, the synods attest that they are bound together in Jesus Christ in a way that transcends existing differences. The declaration then says: "We would increase our guilt towards God and our fellow human beings if we were content with the division. We thank God for the movement of coming together in which we are involved."

Confessional ties with the Protestant tradition as a whole also become a theme, as does the church's overall responsibility for witness and service in the world. The text concludes with the following sentences:

We no longer want to set over against each other the different forms of being church which have taken shape in time, in which we went separate ways, but in obedience to the Lord of the church, we want to introduce them into a process of reunion and renewal.

We pray that our churches, guided by Word and Spirit, may become one church, to the glory of God the Father, in the service of his kingdom.

The notion that different forms of being church could (and should!) be introduced to a process of (re)union and renewal was taken up again in the Declaration of Consensus. A first draft of such a declaration was accepted in 1984 by the synods of the NRC and the RCN and was presented to local congregations and regional assemblies with a request for reactions. The Declaration was finally adopted in 1986 without major changes. This statement became the basis of a formal agreement by the two synods that the NRC and the RCN were "in a state of reunion." This meant that the two churches no longer stood over against each other, although the local congregations' responsibility to determine the nature and tempo of the merger at their level was respected.

The emphasis on the task of (ultimately) becoming one church is important. It seems clear that more than full mutual recognition and intensive collaboration was intended. Nevertheless, little can be inferred from the Declaration regarding relevant aspects of church law. It was not 100 percent clear whether organic union was really necessary or whether, for example, a well-organized federal alliance (that would preserve the churches' separate legal structures) might also be possible.

The purpose of the Declaration of Consensus was to lay the foundations that would make the reunion of the NRC and RCN possible. It is a lengthy document (eleven pages in the report of the joint General Synods) and consists of three parts.

1. The introductory section is short and is marked by the awareness that the common confessional roots of the two churches entail a common obligation. There are no longer differences that separate the denominations. Furthermore, the new questions with which the churches are now being confronted (youth, secularization, and basic life issues) are mentioned as being important motives for unity. We are no longer to waste our energies in endlessly "feeling our way" toward each other.

2. The section entitled "Agreement Shown" deserves more attention. It is interesting that the *Leuenberg Agreement* is not mentioned here at all. That is probably because the two churches have the same confession. Nevertheless, four important themes, which bind the two churches together and provide reasons for closer unity, are addressed. They include the justification of the ungodly, the church as the Body of Christ, the indivisibility of the truth, and the church in service of the kingdom of God. Once we become aware of the deep nature of these matters of faith, the question becomes, can we continue to live like we have so far and still regard issues like "the shape of the Una Sancta," identity, and local independence as reasons for continuing to go our separate ways?

3. The Declaration's third – and longest – part is entitled "Shared Questions." It reflects on five issues, which – from a historical perspective – make the differences between the NRC and the RCN particularly clear. These include church discipline, plurality, "members by birth" (members of the NRC who are not baptized), the relationship between local congregations and the denomination, and public statements by the church. These are important questions for both churches, which can never finally be resolved. Above all, the Declaration attempts to analyze these questions and to clarify the strengths and weaknesses of the answers that have been given by the two churches over the course of a century. These answers have had a theological dimension, but even more significantly, they have often manifested themselves in church practice. In this context, it is pointed out that so far, neither the NRC nor the RCN has formulated a detailed ecclesiology. The relationship between the church and God's covenant or between the church and the kingdom of God has never been identified precisely. There are different

views with respect to such themes in both churches. In light of this, the Declaration emphasizes that a joint way forward can and should be envisioned as a path of shared learning. The renewal of the church, which has already been addressed in the Declaration of Intent, may also manifest itself in joint answers to these questions, however provisional these may need to be.

The request of the synod of the ELC that it be permitted to participate fully in the unification process was on the agenda of the same session of the combi-synod at which the Declaration of Consensus was adopted in November 1986. For several years prior to 1986, the ELC had been included in the process as an observer. At the end of 1985, its synod had come to the conclusion that the ELC could not do justice to its task of proclaiming the gospel unless it was in collaboration with other denominations. The reason for this conclusion was that as a very small church, the ELC was hardly in a position to provide human resources for all of the necessary tasks. The way in which the three churches were bound together by the *Leuenberg Agreement* was recalled in the resolution in which the combi-synod responded positively to the ELC's request.

Since the synod of the ELC had not participated directly in the discussions regarding the Declaration of Consensus, its Theological Commission was asked to give a written reaction. Of course, this also referred to the LA, more formally at the beginning of the response and particularly with regard to our responsibility to the world at the end. Questions about prevailing understandings of Scripture and the church were special themes. The latter topic is relevant here because it is particularly related to questions of church discipline, but the first words of this section are especially interesting:

Lutheranism knows no elaborated doctrine of the church: no single model of the church is preferred above another. The only criterion is and remains the question whether the church is fulfilling its commission to proclaim the gospel. Thus all "feelings about the church" [i.e. unreflective expectations regarding the church, eds.] or "concepts of the church" are of secondary importance.

Between 1986 and 1990, different options for the way forward were considered in reports to the three synods. Would it be preferable to leave the process open-ended and to only intensify mutual cooperation in all areas of church life? In that case, the future would reveal the kind of structures that would be needed. Or was it preferable to work toward a clear goal that would be outlined in a provisional model for the future cooperation of the churches – or the structure of one united church?

2 Towards full unification (1990–2004)

In 1990, the 'trio-synod' (a joint meeting of the three synods involved) made the most important decision in the process: a new church order was to be written. It thus became clear that the path to a complete (organic) union would be pursued.

2.1 The church order process

The structure of the church order was to be based on the NRC's church order. This meant that it would have a relatively short basic constitution; a number of bylaws (ordinances) related to that; additional "transitional regulations;" and some "general regulations" (i.e. lower level legislation). Yet, would it be at all possible to agree on a new church order? There were many doubts. However, in 1993, a Constitution, which specified the ecclesiological and legal outlines of the future church, was accepted by the trio-synod following its first reading. On the basis of that document, the synods had to pass the more specific laws. In the 1990s, other important decisions regarding church order were made. Between 1993 and 2003, the process was dominated by debates on church order, which in the end, did not have a very positive psychological effect on the whole process! This trajectory of exploring church law concluded in June 2003 with the first reading of the Resolution on Union.

During the 1990s, the unification process was mainly characterized by efforts to formulate the aforementioned regulations regarding church order. A joint Church Order Working Group (COWG) composed of representatives from the three churches was engaged in drafting those regulations. Every text first had to be discussed by the trio-synod. Once adopted there, every text had to be discussed and adopted again by a majority vote in each synod acting separately. The next step involved sending the drafts to "minor" ecclesial assemblies on the regional and local levels. Thus, there was ample time for comments. The COWG would then produce a new draft evaluating the comments. After being discussed, possibly amended, and accepted by the trio-synod and the three synods separately, the draft would be final.

After the first reading of the Constitution was completed in 1993, the first reading of the bylaws – fourteen in number – was scheduled for the trio-synod meeting in January 1997. All kinds of matters were regulated by those bylaws. Some examples include the following questions: how are congregations formed; how are officebearers elected; what is the task of the church council; how is a marriage consecrated; and how should the congregation's financial affairs be organized? The participants in the meeting were well prepared. In mixed groups, the members of the synods had already studied the draft of the bylaws between September and December 1996. Their comments had been incorporated into a revised text by the COWG. Thanks to these preparations, a large number of bylaws could be approved without further discussion.

One of the few exceptions to this was the text about the "consecration" of marriages and the "blessing" of "other life relationships" (a term that mainly refers to same-sex relationships). Here the decisive question in a lengthy debate seemed to be whether the same word could and should be used for the involvement of the church in ceremonies involving heterosexual marriages and same-sex unions. The trio-synod decided (with over thirty dissenting votes) that the possibility of blessing (Dutch: *zegenen*) other life relationships would be incorporated into the bylaws, but a proposal to also "bless" marriages (instead of "consecrating" [Dutch: *in*zegenen] them) was not accepted because a majority of the members of the NRC's synod voted against it.

At the request of a number of synod members, the COWG promised that the text of the bylaws would be examined by legal experts on aspects pertaining to civil law. The entire package of bylaws was eventually approved with eighteen dissenting votes. According to the existing rules, these decisions still needed to be ratified at separate synod meetings of the three churches. This happened without further delay. Next, the texts were sent to the classical assemblies and church councils, so that they could give their opinions before the end of 1998. Of course, a large pile of letters with reactions from the regional and local levels was received. The COWG evaluated all of these materials in order to prepare for a final discussion at the trio-synod.

In November 1997, the second debate on the Constitution was on the agenda of the trio-synod. The Constitution, which at that time, included the name United Protestant Church in the Netherlands (UPCN), was accepted with twenty-four dissenting votes (out of almost two hundred). Five

Lutherans and nineteen members of the NRC voted against it. It was a document which was labeled as being "provisionally final." This meant that the text could still be changed (with regard to minor details) if the final discussion of the bylaws gave the trio-synod reason to do so.

The trio-synod needed two full days to discuss each of the nineteen sections of the Constitution. Some minor sections, such as those dealing with objections and disputes, the introduction of changes into the church order, and the church in times of crisis, could be adopted without any discussion. However, most sections required a greater amount of discussion. For instance, there were some very difficult debates regarding the place that the *Leuenberg Agreement* should have in the Constitution. The conservative wing of the synod of the NRC considered the LA to be in direct contradiction to one of the confessions of the NRC and the RCN, namely, the *Dordt Canones*, which is a confessional document rooted in the doctrinal conflict about "double predestination" that erupted in the early seventeenth century. The main problem here can be seen in Article 25 of the LA, which states that "the witness of the Scriptures to Christ forbids us to suppose that God has uttered an eternal decree for the final condemnation of specific individuals or of a particular people." In contrast, for the ELC, the LA had paramount significance as the foundation of its merger with larger Calvinist sister churches. A formulation was found which differed slightly from the original wording of the draft that had been accepted in 1993. That alternative stressed the churches' shared understanding of the gospel, rather than their common acceptance of the LA. Another much debated issue had to do with the question of whether the Constitution should or should not include an article regarding marriage. This discussion did not result in any changes. As before, the Constitution contained a reference to marriage only in the framework of liturgy and not in a separate article on marriage "as instituted by God."

The most difficult issue proved to be the name of the future united church. In 1993, agreement had been reached on the name UPCN, but uneasiness about this name remained, especially in the NRC. The COWG maintained its earlier view that the new name should not contain parts of existing names. Therefore, as an alternative to the "United Protestant Church in the Netherlands," the working group suggested the name "United Reformational Church in the Netherlands" (which had also been proposed, but rejected, in 1993). This proposal did not find any support at the 1997 meeting of the trio-synod and was withdrawn by the COWG. An amendment to accept the name "United Church of the Reformation in the Netherlands (UCRN)" was made from the floor. In Dutch, this would mean that the sound of the name of the NRC could somehow be heard in the new name (Dutch: *"Nederlandse Hervormde Kerk"* and *"Verenigde Kerk van de Hervorming in Nederland"*). Although a majority of the members of the synod of the NRC (forty-five out of around seventy members) voted in favor of UCRN, the majority of the members of the trio-synod rejected this proposal. This gave only nineteen of the aforementioned forty-five members of the trio-synod a reason to reject the Constitution as such in the final vote.

As usual, the decision of the trio-synod to adopt the Constitution needed to be ratified at separate meetings of the synods. The synod of the NRC was the first to meet in March 1998. According to its own rules, this synod could not avoid discussing the whole draft in detail. Again, there were several proposals for other names. During this discussion, the amendment containing the name "The United Church of the Reformation in the Netherlands" was reintroduced. It carried by a small minority of thirty-five to thirty-three votes! All of the other articles of the draft were approved in the form that had been accepted by the trio-synod, but the synod was no longer able to adopt the church order of the future united church. A final vote on the church order could not be taken because the endorsement of another name required additional negotiations with the RCN and the ELC.

The session of the synod of the RCN that met in April 1998 decided to approve the church order in full, including the name "United Protestant Church in the Netherlands." Of course, that synod knew about the decision of the NRC, but it felt that the consequences of different decisions could and should be assessed only after the required procedures had been completed. However, in May 1998, the synod of the ELC voiced its displeasure at the decision of the synod of the NRC. It agreed with a memorandum presented by its board regarding the procedure that had been followed. The synod of the NRC should have consulted with its partners about its desire to find another name, instead of making an abrupt decision, the board said. To the Lutherans, the choice of a name containing the word "Reformation" was evidence that they were not accepted and that the synod of the NRC attached more value to the "historical continuity" of their own church (which was expressed in the name) than it did to the future united church. The synod of the ELC said, "it cannot be our aim to stop the development of the united church. A great deal of good work has already been done, and there are many aspects which join us together. But the union should not be dominated by the toleration of intolerance and the determination to proceed from the primacy of one's own values and point of view, one's own absolute truth." The synods of both the RCN and the ELC included a clause in their decisions which said that their decisions would be valid only if the other synods involved also accepted the same text regarding church order. This kept open the option that the synod of the NRC would eventually decide to agree.

At its session in March 1989, the synod of the NRC also had to deal with other questions and objections regarding the unification process as such. Members of the NRC who had difficulties with the formation of the united church were given until the end of 1998 to submit additional proposals regarding ways to safeguard the identity and legal status of NRC congregations within the future united church. The synod stated emphatically that this decision must not delay the progress of the local and supralocal unification process. As a consequence of this situation, the executive boards of the three churches were responsible for finding a way out of the deadlock. On the one hand, there seemed to be good reasons to take some time to reflect on the situation, while continuing to work on the bylaws, general regulations, and transitional regulations as usual so that no delay would result from the disagreement over the name. On the other hand, the legal situation was such that the synod of the NRC could take a final vote on the Constitution without engaging in new discussions of the whole draft only if this could be done before the end of 1998. In January 1999, twenty percent of the members of the synod would step down, and their successors might legally demand to reopen debate. This might eventually lead to even more points of disagreement between the three synods. That is why the executive boards decided to arrange an extra session of the trio-synod on November 21, 1998.

However, at this meeting, the members of the trio-synod did not manage to achieve a breakthrough in the stalemate surrounding the name that the future united church was to receive. The COWG advised the trio-synod to accept the choice of the synod of the NRC ("United Church of the Reformation in the Netherlands", UCRN), arguing that the term "Reformation" does indeed point to the common roots of both the Calvinist and the Lutheran traditions. It was also stressed that the act of unification would not be worthwhile if it were to cause a major breach in the NRC. However, this proposal was not clearly supported by the three executive boards! At the beginning of the session, each of the three chairpersons made brief introductory remarks. The leadership of the RCN and the ELC made a strong appeal for the members of trio-synod to enter into real dialogue and refrained from offering any specific advice regarding the name to be chosen. The NRC's chairman tried to make the decision of his denomination's synod acceptable by persuading the meeting that there were very strong tensions within the NRC. In fact, these contributions could easily be heard as pleas in favor of the decisions made by the respective synods.

Immediately following these statements, an amendment, which included a proposal to retain the name UPCN, was brought to the floor. During the meeting, many journalists and camera crews were witnesses to what, in fact, was not a discussion, but rather was a long series of monologues. Finally, a majority of 105 out of a total number of nearly 180 delegates voted for the name UPCN, but a majority of the NRC's delegates (48 out of 75 members) voted against it; therefore, the proposal did not pass. Then, the official proposal (UCRN) was voted on, but it also failed to secure a majority because a (large) majority of the members representing the RCN and the ELC voted against it. Thus, the possibility of solving the problems that had emerged before the end of 1998 no longer existed. Furthermore, the ratifying decisions of the synods of the RCN and the ELC had also lost weight because no agreement had yet been reached on the name.

2.2 *The organizational procedure*

In principle, it had already been decided in October of 1996 that all of the national offices of the three churches would be moved to Utrecht. The trio-synod believed that integration of the supra-local organizations of the three denominations was desirable, regardless of their decisions about the new church order. The proposed structure was flexible enough to be adapted if any changes made that necessary. In May 1997, the trio-synod decided to buy part of the former Military Hospital in Utrecht in order to establish the national service center of the joint churches there. Thus, in December 1999, this building became the national office of the three churches. In effect, this meant that there was now one support mechanism for the three churches. In January 1998, the trio-synod accepted a policy document entitled "The church's agenda and the work of its labor organization in 1999–2002."

2.3   The final phase: new tensions

So far, this article might seem to support the view that the unification process was mainly organizational and legal in character, but at the very least,
this would be a one-sided conclusion. Over the years, spiritual and theological issues were introduced into the discussion again and again. For
example, in November 2001, a surprisingly large majority accepted a thorough paper on Christology entitled *Jezus Christus, onze Heer en Verlosser*
(*Jesus Christ, our Lord and Savior*). The final period before the merger
also saw the preparation of new publications on unification itself, which
were designed to promote discussions in local congregations and at ecclesial gatherings about the background and purposes of the unification process. The question of why we were seeking this form of unity was put on
the agenda again. Prayer and the exchange of views had to be stimulated
at the local level.

Around the turn of the century, it became clear that unification would
probably be only a matter of time. No date had been set, and final decisions still had to be made. However, the church order process was making
progress, and the fact that national activities had been totally integrated
into a single organization at least gave the impression that a point of no
return was close. As was to be expected, this state of affairs exacerbated
internal tensions within the individual churches.

2.3.1   Tensions in the NRC

The situation in the NRC was by far the most complicated. Partly due to
secularization and a decrease in the number of members, the more conservative and orthodox wing of this church had gained more influence over
time and was not unconditionally in favor of unification, to say the least.
Part of this group was even unconditionally against the merger and eventually threatened to leave the NRC. There were various reasons for this, but
the most important ones included the following:
– In terms of doctrine, there were problems with the inclusion of the
  Leuenberg Agreement in the Constitution. As mentioned above, the LA –
  which, in the interim, had come to have major ecumenical significance
  in Europe – holds that the classic doctrinal conflicts between the Reformed and Lutheran traditions have been transcended by a new common understanding of the gospel. Those conflicts no longer have the
  power to divide churches. This assessment provided a theological basis

for the unification process, but conservative members of the NRC saw it as denying the importance of the doctrine of predestination.

– From a more materialistic point of view, there were huge tensions within the NRC concerning the say that the church as a whole had with regard to the properties of local congregations. A process designed to arrive at uniform internal rules of church order regarding this matter (which was also undertaken because of the unification process) had led to a number of civil court cases. In all of those, the church as a whole was judged to be right, but of course, that fact could not prevent bitterness.

– For part of the NRC constituency, another issue was the idea that the NRC was – in unbroken continuity – the "church of the Netherlands," that is, the church that had been founded by the first Christian missionaries to the area, such as Saint Willibrord and Saint Boniface in the seventh century CE. This church was regarded as "having gone through the Reformation" and as continuing to exist in the NRC. It was believed that this continuity should be expressed in the name of the future united church. This was one of the reasons that the name "Uniting Protestant Church in the Netherlands" was rejected.

– A major difficulty was related to the issue of marriage and same-sex relationships. As stated above, the draft version of the bylaw on worship included the option for a local church council to facilitate (under strict conditions) the act of blessing same-sex relationships during worship services. The conservative part of the church saw this as "condoning what God condemns." The draft text had been accepted by the synod of the NRC, but only by a small majority of forty to thirty-three.

For these and other reasons, there had been repeated efforts in recent years to compel the NRC's synod to express support for a less far-reaching mode of unification in which the three churches would continue their separate existence, while cooperating very intensively in a "federation model." In June 2002, the synod of the NRC again rejected such a proposal by a vote of twenty-three to fifty. By June 1997, the NRC had already included a rule in its own constitution which stipulated that at least a two-thirds majority of the votes cast would be required for the final decision to unite with the RCN and the ELC to be ratified. Prior to that, the NRC's constitution had not included a specific "unification clause."

2.3.2 Tensions in the RCN

For a long time, it had seemed that there were no significant tensions within the RCN. Serious problems did not become manifest until the year 2000. The RCN had always been a "confederative" denomination in which the local congregation (rather than the denomination) was the basic entity in legal terms. If, for instance, a local church council, supported by a majority of the congregation's constituency, were to identify serious theological or confessional objections to the synod's policies, it might even decide to leave the denomination. In such a case, the members of the congregation could take the properties of the local church with them. In 2000, it became obvious that such decisions would no longer be possible under the law of the future united church. The relationship between congregation and denomination would be the same as it was in the NRC. Of course, people could leave the PCN, but the congregation, as a legal entity with a corporate personality, would continue to be part of the church. Properties would belong to this legal entity and could not be taken from that body.

The synod of the RCN sent a report to the local congregations, assessing this analysis of the future church order and asking for comments. The number of objections that this report raised had never been seen before! Many church councils expressed the feeling that, although they saw no reason whatsoever to leave the church at that moment, this option should remain in the future church law as a matter of principle. New regulations were prepared to address the objections as much as possible. Such transitional provisions were intended to reduce tensions for at least the first few years. A procedure was included in church law so that an independent church court could render a decision regarding church properties in cases where (larger parts of) congregations opted to leave the church. This restored confidence that the synod of the RCN eventually would wholeheartedly agree with the decision to unite.

In many respects, the draft of the new church order for the PCN was close to the NRC's existing church order. This was not the case with the RCN's church order. This fact led the synod of the RCN to make some changes in its own church order so that the transition to unification would be smoother. For instance, it decided that the 'particular synods' (i.e. assemblies composed of representatives of classes in a region) should no longer be represented at the general synods; rather, the classes themselves would be represented at those meetings. A procedure was agreed upon according to which the synod of the RCN would make the decisions about unification, which would include the right of local churches to express their opinions regarding the final proposal. The administration of justice in the RCN did not meet the standards that are currently laid down to ensure effective legal protection. The RCN did not have independent church courts; church assemblies adjudicated conflicts themselves. Thus, the rules for "objections and disputes" that were developed for the UPCN (and were quite similar to those of the NRC), were partially introduced into the RCN's church order.

2.3.3 Tensions in the ELC

The issue of same-sex relationships was crucial for the Lutherans, too, but for opposite reasons. For them, the acceptance of homosexual members and opportunities for them to receive a liturgical blessing was decisive. In recent decades, this church (and other small denominations) had made decisions about this matter that could not be given up.

Although there was fear in some congregations that the Lutheran tradition would be washed away by the huge Reformed majority in the future united church, the general view was that the Lutheran synod would continue to support the unification process by a large majority. However, it was also clear that the long-term process and large number of discussions needed were creating increasingly greater difficulties for the Lutherans. They feared that they would run out of human resources. Thus, a faster pace in the process was favored.

2.4 Concentration

With the most important texts ready, the moment of unification was coming quite close. In April 2002, the joint board of the trio-synod decided to design a timetable for the final phase of the unification process. A decision to intensify the unification process was made. All available resources were to be used to complete it as soon as possible. This was deemed to be necessary because the long-lasting process was producing more and more negative effects: growing alienation, self-absorption, diminishing patience on the local level, reduced confidence and commitment among those in favor of unification, growing confusion, and so on. The date of December 12, 2003 was set for the synods' final decision on unification, but several steps had to be taken in a period of twenty months. One of them involved giving adequate information to all of the congregations regarding the anticipated final stage of the process. In a lengthy letter, the joint board addressed all of the major issues in an attempt to adequately meet the concerns of those who were hesitant about these decisive developments. Most of the issues that the letter dealt with were related to questions regarding the extent to which a local congregation would be entitled to develop a specific identity. Different concerns in this area had been expressed by the three participating churches on the basis of their particular historical experiences.

The COWG had completed most of its activities by September 2002. All of the drafts were ready by then, including a number of detailed technical regulations and the "transitional regulations" that were needed to facilitate a smooth transition from three old church orders to one new church order. The trio-synod decided on most of these in November and December 2002. Only a few regulations had to be reconsidered and brought before the trio-synod again in June 2003. Some financial and organizational matters required new administrative structures, and changes in theological education, which had to be made due to governmental measures, needed to be dealt with in the church law as well.

By the end of 2002, the issue of the name of the church was also on the agenda again; now a decision would finally have to be made. The board of the trio-synod adopted a report that identified four criteria. The name should (a) express continuity with the common tradition and (b) be appealing (that is, it should be more than an administrative compromise). It should (c) not easily be confused with the names of other churches in the Netherlands, and it should (d) not include any element that was definitive for the name of one of the three uniting churches. Furthermore, the joint board did not want to propose a name that had been voted on at an earlier stage of the process. The name "Protestant Church in the Netherlands" met all of these criteria. Thus, it was proposed by the joint board and accepted by a session of the trio-synod in November 2002.

In the aforementioned report, ample attention was given to the historical content and current potential of the word "protestant." Historically, it refers to the "Protestation" advocating freedom of religion which was carried out in Spiers, Germany, on *Reichstag* (Empire Day) in 1529 by a number of princes and cities that were in favor of the Reformation. The Latin verb *"protestari"* – unlike the English verb "to protest" and the Dutch verb *"protesteren"* – has a meaning that is basically positive: "to witness publicly." A majority of the people backing the Protestation were Lutherans, but Reformed cities like Strasbourg (Martin Bucer) were also intensely involved. Thus, historically speaking, it is possible to understand "Protestant" as referring to a church that is primarily called to witness publicly to the gospel in Dutch society. As to the potential that this word has to speak in this time, much will depend on the way that the Protestant Church in the Netherlands takes its place in our society. The meanings and associations connected with the Dutch word "*protestants*" will gradually be determined by the performance of this particular church on both the national and local levels. The name could also be viewed as an invitation to other Dutch Protestant denominations to cooperate – and perhaps to unite – with the Protestant Church in the Netherlands in due time.

After agreeing on the name of the church, the three individual synods could formally make a final decision regarding the Constitution of the Protestant Church in the Netherlands, and so they did! Most of the bylaws were adopted as well.

During the first six months of 2003, it became crucial to clearly distinguish among three different levels of the process. First, in the context of finalizing the process, a fresh consideration of the theological nature of unification was needed. Any impression that the merger was only meant to be an administrative matter had to be avoided. For that purpose, the board of the trio-synod prepared a draft entitled Declaration on Unification. Secondly, meticulous procedures had to be developed to meet the specific legal requirements of each of the three uniting churches. For instance, each church order included rules designed to involve the grass-roots level of the churches in the final decisions, but these rules were different for each of the churches. This situation had to be taken seriously during the final stage in order to keep the final decision from being vulnerable to judicial proceedings afterwards. Thirdly, civil law has its own requirements in cases involving a unification of churches. People and legal entities, both inside and outside of the churches, had to be given optimal clarity and guarantees with respect to the rights, responsibilities, and claims that they might have. This would apply to issues like the legal relationship between a local congregation and the church as a whole; the pension rights of retired ministers; the church's obligations to banks with regard to mortgages; and so forth.

A proposal that included the draft version of the Declaration on Unification and decisions in the area of church and civil law had to be discussed at the trio-synod meeting in June 2003. That body adopted the draft of the declaration with only minor changes. That declaration – which contains about 400 words – expresses thankfulness to God and faith in Jesus Christ "who prayed for the unity of his Church" and is the one "in whom we can only find our unity." It says that "we would increase our guilt if we would acquiesce in our separations." It refers to the vulnerability that character-izes the unity of the churches and speaks of the continuing need for true reconciliation "at the foot of the Cross." Finally, it focuses on the church's vocation "to be present in society, in witness and service," as well as on the on-going call for it to seek wider unity with other churches. It ends with a prayer: "Come, Holy Spirit, renew your church."

Furthermore, in a set of quite complicated and detailed formulations, the trio-synod asked each of the individual synods to make final decisions regarding church and civil law that would specifically address the require-ments mentioned above. This was the last action required of the trio-synod. From now on, each of the churches had to act separately, according to its own procedures, to prepare for the final decision that was to be made on December 12, 2003. In this final round, it was up to the congregations and/or the regional assemblies to present their views on unification to their respective synods.

In 2003, the new logo of the future Protestant Church in the Nether-lands was presented. It consists of an orange, red, and yellow circle with a white cross and a white dove at its heart. The circle symbolizes unity and also refers to God as the beginning and the end. The cross does not need an explanation. In the center, we see a dove, a sign of peace and symbol of the Holy Spirit. Altogether, the logo reminds us of the Triune God.

2.5 Final decisions

During the final months of 2003, expectations – as well as concerns – were growing. From the outset, there was great confidence that the synod of the RCN would vote to unite with the NRC and the ELC by a large majority that would far exceed the required two-thirds margin. However, more doubts existed with regard to the synod of the NRC, where a two-thirds major-ity also had to be found. If, in the end, all of the "pending" votes were negative, unification might fail as a result of just a few votes out of the total number of seventy-five. On the local level, quite a few of the more conservative congregations continued to express strong doubts about the legitimacy of unification with the Lutherans, mainly due to fear of a liberal sort of "plurality," but also partially as the result of a more specific view, which supposed that it was God's providential will that the Dutch church be Reformed. There continued to be fears that these congregations would not be permitted to shape their lives according to the Reformed confession.

In order to provide optimal clarity, the board of the synod of the NRC sent a lengthy letter to all of the congregations, stressing the fact that according to the PCN's Constitution, local congregations would not be compelled to unite or to modify their identities. Moreover, in the bylaws (ordinances), Reformed congregations were said to have a "special commitment to the confessional standards of the Reformed tradition." In addition, the Constitution identified Holy Scripture as being "the one source and norm of the church's proclamation and ministry." This statement should stimulate an ongoing search for a common understanding of the gospel. A Reformed congregation would be entitled to maintain a strict interpretation of its "special commitment" to Reformed confessional standards, for example, by focusing on them fully in proclamation and catechesis. However, it would not be acceptable to deny the legitimacy of Lutheran congregations within the Protestant Church in the Netherlands. Finally, the letter from the board of the NRC's synod provided the option for a local congregation to explicitly indorse (and include in its rules) a declaration which, among other things, stated the following:

- The congregation had not agreed with a number of the synods' decisions regarding unification.
- It would continue to champion its own understanding of obedience to the Holy Scriptures.
- It had committed itself to the Reformed tradition.
- On the basis of its understanding of Holy Scripture, it rejected certain options that the Church Order of the PNC leaves to the choice of individual congregations (like allowing children to partake of the Lord's Supper or accepting ceremonies that bless the unions of same-sex couples).

By the fall of 2003, there were clear indications that about sixty of the seventy-five members of the synod of the NRC would approve the proposed unification.

Beforehand, the situation in the ELC had been judged to be the most challenging. The synod of the ELC consisted of thirty-six members, and according to its church law, a three-fourths majority was required to approve the merger. It was known that six members of the synod would reject the proposal, and it was possible that four (or more) others might join them. If that were to happen, the unification would fail.

On Friday December 12, separate synod meetings were held at the same time at different church buildings in the city of Utrecht. As expected, the synod of the RCN recorded six votes against unification out of a total of seventy-five. At the synod of the ELC, the negative votes were limited to the six members who were already known to be against the merger, so unification was not in jeopardy there either. However, the final vote of the synod of the NCR was really tight. Nevertheless, with fifty-one votes in favor and twenty-four against, the proposal was accepted in accordance with the legal requirements!

In keeping with its responsibilities, the board of the trio-synod had prepared two scenarios. If the unification were to fail, all of the members of the synods would be expected to meet at one of the churches in the evening for a service of prayer and humility. In the other case, a service of thanksgiving was to be held in the (now Reformed/Protestant) Dom Church, which formerly was the Minster Church of the Roman Catholic archbishop in the Netherlands, the successor to Willibrord who was bishop from 695 to 739. So it happened! Her Majesty Queen Beatrix attended the service, along with ecumenical guests from many partner churches in the national Council of Churches and many church members who came to the church spontaneously.

At the start of the service, the chairpersons and secretaries of the three synods put their signatures beneath a formal Declaration on Unification, which reads:

Today, December 12th, 2003,
the General Synod of the Netherlands Reformed Church
the General Synod of the Reformed Churches in the Netherlands
and the Synod of the Evangelical Lutheran Church in the Kingdom of the Netherlands
decided to unite the churches which are entrusted to their care and guidance into the Protestant Church in the Netherlands.

We unite believing that *our Lord Jesus Christ* himself prayed for the unity of his Church, so that the world may believe in Him.
The separate roads which our churches in the Netherlands have been following since the Reformation in the 16th century and the two secessions in the 19th century, meet here.

In recent years the churches have been 'together on the way' with the purpose to unite. In decisions and declarations, and especially in accepting the church order of the Protestant Church in the Netherlands, our longing for unity has gradually taken shape.

We pray for renewal by the *Holy Spirit* and express
– our confidence that the Spirit will continue to lead his Church
– our desire to proclaim the Name of our Lord and to give expression to his love and faithfulness in Dutch society
– our hope that – where concerns continue to exist within the church – we may find each other in the name of our Lord
– our willingness to continue seeking a growing visible unity of God's Church in the future.

Soli Deo Gloria

After that, gratitude and joy were expressed in prayers and songs. Nevertheless, in his sermon on Romans 5:5–6 (which was the Epistle reading for that week according to our common *Book of Worship*), the Rev. Dr. Bas Plaisier, who had been elected the General Secretary of the Protestant Church in the Netherlands, rightly said: "We are sitting here, in dignity, rather than in exaltation. We are grateful, but with a certain measure of restraint. It is as if we still cannot believe that it has really happened." Again, and stronger than before, the mood of the service was most recognizable in the prayer: "Come, Holy Spirit, renew your church!"

The same evening, a message, which was to be read during all worship services on Sunday, December 14, was distributed electronically. It began by expressing gratitude and resolve with regard to the church's mandate to witness to Jesus Christ. It also spoke of the need for everyone in the church to experience the space and respect that are essential to being the church of Jesus Christ together. Paul's appeal was recalled: "Welcome one another, therefore, as Christ has welcomed you, for the glory of God" (Romans 15:7).

The decisions that were made on December 12 included the final adoption of the set of "transitional regulations" that guided the process of implementing the merger. The old separated church bodies and assemblies had to conclude their activities so that they could be dissolved; new bodies and assemblies had to be elected; and so forth. In March 2004, the final session of the (old) trio-synod was convened, and this was immediately followed by the final separate sessions of the three synods. Apart from some legally necessary decisions, the emphasis was placed on reflection, evaluation, and sharing memories of the past.

After that, an initial (provisional) meeting of the synod of the Protestant Church in the Netherlands was held to elect new officers and appoint the members of a number of the church's national committees. Thus, all of the arrangements had been made to prepare for the formal birth of the Protestant Church in the Netherlands on May 1, 2004. During the final weeks of April, 2004, the board of the synod sent a letter to all of the congregations with a request that they take note of the unification during their worship services on Sunday, May 2, 2004. On the eve of May 1 – that is on April 30, which happened to be Queen's Day (the main annual national holiday) – the formal deed of legal unification was signed in the presence of a notary public in the context of a celebrative meeting of many of the people who had been strongly involved in the unification process on a national level during the preceding decades. The board of the synod again published a statement, expressing gratitude, hope, commitment, and confidence.

The first formal session of the General Synod of the Protestant Church in the Netherlands was convened within a few weeks from May 12 to 14, 2004. Many representatives of ecumenical bodies and partner churches – both from the national context and the global level – attended as guests. These participants shared in the festivities and in intense discussions of the vision that the Protestant Church in the Netherlands had of its mission for the years to come.

2.6 Consequences

It was clear from the outset – as has been the case with most "organic unions" throughout the world – that not everyone would remain part of the Protestant Church in the Netherlands. The ELC joined without further divisions. In the RCN, 8 out of nearly 850 congregations used their legal right to opt out; they provisionally formed the "Continued Reformed Churches in the Netherlands," although one of them joined the Protestant Church in the Netherlands within a year. NRC congregations had no option to leave the NRC *as legal entities*, but altogether about 60,000 members (out of some 1.5 million) decided to leave the church, usually in groups, splitting local congregations. In quite a few cases, civil law proceedings were begun to reclaim church properties. Transitional regulations in the church law included a procedure for these kinds of situations. National committees of the Protestant Church in the Netherlands, which were called "committees of special care," were set up in an attempt to maintain as much communication as possible with those who were opposed to the unification. The mandate of these committees included the authority to transfer church properties to groups that were leaving the church in cases where that would be necessary for a separate community to start. In light of these regulations, civil courts rejected all of the aforementioned claims, urging the parties involved to first deal with the committees of special care before suing the church in courts of civil law.

During the first twenty months of the existence of the Protestant Church in the Netherlands, plenary sessions of the General Synod dealt with a number of issues that are regarded as being decisive for the role of the church in Dutch society. Included among these were "the missional aspects of church life," "the future agenda of synod," and the "multicultural society" (May 2004); the "diaconia" (September 2004); "youth and the church" (November 2004); the "training of local ministers and pastoral care in health institutions" (April 2005); and the Accra Confession entitled *Covenanting for Justice in the Economy and the Earth*, which was adopted by the General Assembly of the World Alliance of Reformed Churches (September 2004 and November 2005).

In October 2004, the first Dutch ecumenical translation of the Bible was published! From the outset, this was received very positively. The General Synod of the Protestant Church in the Netherlands authorized it for use in worship, and many congregations immediately followed this recommendation. The general public gave this *Nieuwe Bijbelvertaling* the prestigious honor of being selected "Book of the Year" in 2005. At its meeting in September 2005, the General Synod of the PCN discussed and accepted a vision statement entitled *Leren leven van de verwondering* (Learning to live out of wonder; see below, 40). This report is intended to guide groups, committees, and individuals at all levels of the church who want to be involved in a process of discussing priorities for the future life of the church. The main thrust of this booklet is to eradicate feelings of pessimism so that the church can live from the power of biblical hope in a changing society, both in the Netherlands and on a global scale.

3 Evaluative remarks

The significance of the unification is still a matter for the future to decide. Was it an end, or rather, a new beginning? The bylaw on ecumenical relations introduces an opportunity for churches and congregations outside of the PCN to relate to the denomination as an "associated" church or congregation. Some migrant churches have, in fact, opted for association. This has made it possible for them to share at all of the appropriate levels and to have the right to vote at the General Synod. In the long run, this could change the very white and very western face that the church has had so far.

On December 12, 2005, Dr. Ton van Eijk, a Roman Catholic ecumenical theologian and the chairperson of the Council of Churches in the Netherlands, addressed a commemorative gathering that was convened exactly two years after the final decisions about unification had been made. He reflected on the ecumenical impact of the birth of the Protestant Church in the Netherlands, acknowledging the importance of unity, not only in terms of communion in Word and sacrament (including a common *Book of Worship*), but also in terms of the organic unity represented by the PCN's common structure and organization within one general synod. From an ecumenical point of view, he saw the unification and reconciliation of churches from the Lutheran and Reformed traditions into one denomination as being more significant than the unification and reconciliation of the two Reformed churches.

Another speaker was the well-known philosopher Professor Kees Klop. Dr. Klop focused on the potential role of the Protestant Church in the Netherlands in Dutch society. He emphasized that openness to new developments, which is directly related to the traditional Protestant stress on the individual person, *coram Deo*, is one of Protestantism's most important features. In his opinion, this ability to meet new challenges has had a major impact on Dutch society as a whole throughout the course of history and has the potential to do so in the future as well – if Protestantism presents itself with confidence. Dr. Klop concluded his comments with the following statement: "The birth of the PCN is in itself significant in this respect. It proves that emphasizing the significance of the individual person does not necessarily lead toward a relativizing of the community, ongoing fragmentation and separation; it can just as well foster the revitalization of a community."

By now, it should be clear that *unity* is a complicated concept. What kind of unity do we seek? This question has to be reconsidered again and again. Other questions lie behind it. Why are we so focused on organic unity? What exactly is decisive for our unity: only church order or also real communion in confessing our faith together? In many respects, the PCN is a roof over a large variety of congregations, representing a number of different spiritual approaches. The need to ensure a safe haven for these congregations – where they can continue their existence without being threatened or challenged – seems to be more important than the desire to deepen communication between various theological and confessional streams. The challenge of developing mutual accountability within the larger body continues to be relevant.

As stated above, the unification process started from a *mission* perspective in 1962. Fifty years later, the world is quite different. The Netherlands is highly secularized. The majority of its inhabitants say that they do not to belong to any church, although statistics regarding church attendance are significantly higher than they are in most Western European countries! A postmodern attitude and mood dominates culture – which hardly shows any interest in ecclesial institutions, but, at the same time, reacts to the existence of a variety of denominations in a much less negative way.

Uncertainty about exactly what is decisive for the *identity* of the united church might be at the core of all of the questions and problems. Is identity primarily related to the confessional foundation of a church? Or is identity mainly a matter of the provisions and structures specified in the church order? Is it organic unity as such? Is it primarily provided by a common presbyterial-synodal church order? Or is a common *Book of Worship* (which includes a rich variety of options) like the one the PCN adopted a decade ago decisive? Or can the identity of the church finally be found only outside of itself in Jesus Christ, our Lord and Savior? That has to be said, and it has to be affirmed, but it does not answer all of the questions.

Abbreviations and bibliography

COWG: Church Order Working Group.
ELC: Evangelical Lutheran Church in the Kingdom of the Netherlands.
LA: Leuenberg Agreement (1973).
NRC: Netherlands Reformed Church.
PCN: Protestant Church in the Netherlands.

RCN: Reformed Churches in the Netherlands.

UCRN: United Church of the Reformation in the Netherlands.

UPCN: United Protestant Church in the Netherlands.

Best, Thomas F. (ed.). 2002. Survey of Church Union Negotiations 1999–2002. Faith and Order Paper 192. Geneva: WCC.

Best, Thomas F. (ed.). 2004. With a Demonstration of the Spirit and of Power: Seventh International Consultation of United and Uniting Churches. Faith and Order Paper 195. Geneva: WCC.

Protestant Church in the Netherlands. 2000. Jesus Christ, our Lord and Saviour. Accessed February 12, 2014. http://www.unitingprotestantchurches.nl.

The Heartbeat of the Life of the Protestant Church in the Netherlands

Arjan Plaisier

The merger of three churches into the Protestant Church in the Netherlands required considerable effort. The forty years that it took have often been compared to the length of time that the Israelites spent wandering through the desert. If we continue to think of that story, the question automatically arises regarding whether the unification has brought us into a promised land in which church members and congregation are enjoying a blessed time. It will not come as a surprise to anyone who is familiar with contemporary church life if this question elicits a negative response. Nevertheless, ten years after the unification, we can look back and conclude that it was worth the effort and that we have indeed entered a new land. The church division existing between two denominations of the same "Calvinist branch" – which the well-known Dutch theologian Arnold A. van Ruler († 1970) called a "quarrel about household questions" – has worn out itself. We still find differences within our united church. However, only a limited number of these differences have to do with past tensions between the *Nederlandse Hervormde Kerk* and the *Gereformeerde Kerken in Nederland* – even though not all congregations of the former denominations have united on a local level. This is also the case with a considerable number of Evangelical Lutheran congregations that have not yet united with a congregation of the Calvinistic tradition, although there often is some sort of cooperation between these congregations.

The first vision paper

The church unification was the end of a long process. It was also a new beginning in a time that is not favorable to the church. The Protestant Church in the Netherlands began its life at a time when secularization had considerable influence – which may even be increasing – in the Netherlands. Compared with other Western European countries, the Netherlands probably is the most secularized country. This has had and still has consequences for church membership. The PCN's total number of members has declined by 2.5 % every year during these ten years, and the present number is less than the membership of the former *Nederlandse Hervormde Kerk* in 1980.

In the light of this phenomenon, but also because of other challenges, the PCN had – from the very beginning – to face the question of what kind of church it was and wanted to be. What vision did it have of itself and its place in Dutch society? What priorities needed to be set? What emphases should be accentuated? Questions like these cannot be evaded, not only because the PCN is a new reality, but also, and especially, because the church's existence is no longer a story that will continue automatically, as it was in the time of the *corpus Christianum*.

Shortly after the birth of the Protestant Church in the Netherlands, a vision paper entitled *Learning to Live out of Wonder* was prepared and approved by the General Synod. This vision paper is meant to express what the PCN is all about and what targets it wants to reach in the coming years. It is not a confession of faith or a piece of theological literature; rather, it is a short, powerful, inspiring text, which is intended to guide the policies and plans that the church will draw up in the coming years. In 2005, the most remarkable feature of *Learning to Live out of Wonder* was the concept of the church in mission. Nowadays, this is a common notion in the church, and perhaps the term "mission" has been inflated a bit. However, ten years ago, accentuating this aspect of church life came as something of a surprise. In addition, stress was placed on the importance of the participation of youth in the life of the church. These two emphases had consequences for the strategy of the service center of the PCN. Two new key departments were set up: a Youth Department and a Mission Department. Between 2009 and 2013, two "mission tours" were organized. In each of these, around fifty locations were visited in an effort to challenge local congregations to think about the church's mission agenda. A loose-leaf folder with thirty models for doing mission was provided to help congregations think about their own mission style.

Time moves quickly, and after 5 years, the need for follow-up was felt. Thus, a new vision paper was prepared and approved by the Synod in November 2011. It is called *The Heartbeat of Life, a Vision Paper for the Life and Work of the Protestant Church in the Netherlands (Heartbeat)*.

The situation

Although *Learning to Live* had a favorable reception, questions were raised regarding whether it had taken sufficient account of the crisis in church life on both the general and local levels. Thus, *Heartbeat* was prepared only after visits had been made to a wide range of congregations and boards of the regional bodies of the church that are known as "classical assemblies." This "tour" made it clear that a general picture of local church life cannot be sketched. The team encountered congregations that had a conventional church life and places where new initiatives were being taken and clear enthusiasm was evident. In other places, church life was weak; the youth had vanished from the church community; and there were serious difficulties filling vacant positions on the local church council. The overall impression was that of a church in poor health. The team was particularly struck by a kind of hesitance that was apparent when congregations were asked "why the church?" This hesitation became even more pronounced when the question was "why believe in God?" Taking all of these impressions to heart, we tried to formulate four main issues – four emphases or conclusions – that may speak to the present situation. In the following pages, I will describe these emphases.

Back to the roots

The main theme in *Heartbeat* is the classic Protestant principle "back to the roots." Particularly in a late modern or postmodern situation in which there is a feeling of being part of an archaic Christianity and an outdated church, it is good to be back in touch with the living origins of the Church. Going back to the roots is not to be done for nostalgic reasons, as a wistful look back at the pure phase of the first congregation. Going back to the roots is motivated by the fact that the church did not start with us; it began with a movement that came "from above" and gave rise to the church. Perhaps our problem with the church is that this creative origin is constantly being forgotten.

Going back to the origins also means getting a renewed vision – a new image – of the church. In this case, this image will not be a sheer invention, only a product of our intuition or creative imagination. First and foremost, it will involve rediscovering what we are as a church, what makes the church, or better yet, *who* makes the church. Although we do not invent the church, going back to the roots is still a creative process. Going back to the roots means that the crisis in which the church finds itself cannot be overcome by a strategy, a "trick," or even by a clever program of church engineering. It can only be overcome by living as the church again. This will be possible only by our "being made church" again, and that is not in our hands; it is in the Lord's hand. Nevertheless, this will not happen unless we once again realize what the church is, to whom the church belongs, and how we may live that reality. That is the reason for the movement back to the roots.

Content

This image automatically leads to the first emphasis or conclusion. The church is the Body of Christ. It starts with Christ, who is the risen Lord. We can compare the present human situation with that of the disciples who gathered behind closed doors, perhaps engaged in a discussion regarding which of them would blow out the candle before going home (see John 20:19). That was the very moment that the risen Christ entered with the greeting "peace be with you." This scene creates the church and gives content to the church. Christ is the gift of God, and the church is the gift of Christ. The word and presence of the living Christ are the sole origin and foundation of the church. There never was a project called "Church" that was disseminated throughout the world. People came together on the day of the resurrection believing that Christ was in their midst. Thus, the current crisis is a problem, but it is not a mortal problem. We always come with empty hands and live by virtue of the surprise of the gospel and the living Lord who still loves us and gives himself to us. This time of crisis is a time to realize that the church is not the result of our efforts; it is totally a gift from God.

It is very important to *live* this reality! To receive Christ and to respond to his gift with acceptance and confession. We are not called to remain in our dumbness, shyness, or embarrassment and confusion. Perhaps there was a necessary phase in our history during which there was a breakdown of a type of Christianity that was too confident in itself. There may have been a time when the certainties of the past, rather than our trust in the

Lord, seemed to be our certainties. Those certainties have broken down and must be given up. Nevertheless, a church lives by faith. A church that is vague about its faith will come to an end. Thus, it is important to practice this faith and to be an authentic witness to it.

It is a strange phenomenon that we talk about everything in the life of the church, but only rarely speak about our faith in God, our experience with Christ, and how we walk with God. Too often, we "do" our services in the proper liturgical order (which, of course, is commendable), as a type of religious duty, and leave it there. Thus, we are in need of conversations about faith and groups that read the Bible together and discuss its significance for one another and our lives. We also need to develop additional mission courses in order to transmit the Christian faith to the next generation and to people who are seriously searching for the meaning of life and spirituality.

Form

A church does not exist as an invisible kind of spirit; rather it is a body. It has a concrete form. What kind of form? It may be useful for us to go back to the most basic form of church life. The verse from the Gospel of Matthew where Jesus says, "For where two or three gather in my name, there am I with them" functioned as a trigger for the development of a vision of the church's form (Matthew 18:20, NRSV). A church is a fellowship of people who live together in Christ's name. It is that simple. In times of crises and the loss of many facilities, this awareness can help a lot. Church life does not depend on buildings or existing structures. The highly developed forms of church life can even obscure the basic form, which is "Christ with his disciples." To quote the vision paper: "Sometimes it becomes less: less people, less ministers, less money. That hurts. And nevertheless that can give a view of the real 'more:' the living Word of the Lord, the nearness of a God of love who gives us to each other."

Now and then, this ground plan of the church is overgrown by a thousand activities and "musts." Church becomes a full agenda. It is a total package of services and responsibilities. Fewer and fewer people are given more and more tasks, and they almost groan under the burden. Where is the joy of being together in Jesus' name when the church becomes an organization that has to be run by us? Maybe this is the time to make things simpler; to once again make clear what a congregation is: a fellowship of faith.

The church has acquired its forms through a process of cultivating tradition. That is good and significant. Yet, it cannot be denied that such forms often are well suited to the mainstream culture of "yesterday." What about the church's accessibility to the people of today's culture? There needs to be a reconsideration of form and the freedom to experiment with new forms. Not as a simple trick, but as a way for "the Word to be made flesh" through a type of "inculturalization" of the church in contemporary life. For that reason, the PCN has already started "pioneer congregations." This idea has been expanded in the new policy guidelines. There will be an opportunity for 100 pioneer sites to be established between 2013 and 2017. The Mission Department will coach and encourage members of the church as they seek to develop these places. About twenty possible sites outside of regular church settings have been approved. This is a way of fostering "fresh expressions of church." Time will reveal whether this approach will succeed, but I think it is a courageous endeavor that demonstrates our commitment to being a church for this generation and the next. We are convinced that the Reformed type of church order is not a stiff harness; it is a supple garment that is flexible enough to enable experiments.

Part of the "form" involves reflections on church buildings. The PCN is the proud possessor of hundreds of churches, which include a fairly large number of historic churches. It is impossible to maintain all of them. Church buildings sometimes have to be handed over for demolition or to be sold. This has a deep impact on members, and even on people who live near the buildings. Perhaps building churches was too booming a business during the period after the Second World War; thus, many of these churches now have to be given up. Nevertheless, church buildings play an important role. They have a symbolic and functional *raison d'être*, and in many situations, there are a number of reasons to keep a building. On the national level, we are trying to start an organization which, under certain conditions, will agree to take over a building with the guarantee that the local congregation can still make use of it.

A Church for others

The church is, by definition, an open church. It is open because God calls people from all backgrounds to share in the life of Christ. It is open because the church is sent into the "world." Of course, that is a big word. What does it mean? What is the church's significance for others and for its setting? In *Heartbeat*, we came to the conclusion that before beginning a list of practical suggestions, it must be stressed that it is the church itself which is significant. Here, church is viewed as a community of people who live together in Christ's name. What was the gift that the early church gave to the ancient world? It was the church itself – as a community in which people were reconciled to God and to each other. It was a community in which Jesus Christ was confessed to be the Lord and other lordships were relativized.

In spite of the great value that is given to individualism in today's society, people are desperately longing for a real community. A community in which violence is overcome, enmity reconciled, and solidarity practiced, not in the name of an ideal or an interest, but in the name of love. If there was no church, a church would be invented, but, in fact, there is a church. There is a community, not as a result of human bargaining or organizing but thanks to the Holy Spirit. The church is a place where people are constantly called back to its roots and summoned to be a reconciled community. This cannot occur unless the sin of not being reconciled is confessed. There are many reasons to do this. Only by confessing our sins – not only to God but also to each other – do we learn what it means to be a reconciled community. In this way, the church can be a sign to the nation and a source of hope to people who would otherwise fall asunder, and become atomic individuals. The church is open to all; thus, it needs to have the courage to invite people to become members. Up to now, we have been more focused on "our own folk" and have lacked the drive to really welcome new members.

Of course, this community is not only open in the sense that it invites everyone to participate in its life; it is also a community that is sent to everyone. It is called to practice its life in Christ. This means keeping an eye open for people who are in need, both within the community and outside of it. Particularly at a time when the government is receding and the welfare state is in retreat, it is important to think about how the church can act in a relevant way. The diaconia is a vital part of the church's identity. Remembering what was said earlier about "form," it is important to set priorities. It would be a pitfall to try to prove our relevance by filling the gap that the government has left open. Churches should do what they can, and accept the fact that it is limited. They should look for partners in the field and work together wherever possible. In other words, let your heart speak and do what you can.

A church that sees itself as a community is a church which lives a particular ethos. Without giving cheap answers, it helps people find a way of life amidst the complexities of everyday existence. On the basis of community life, there can be a consideration of ethical themes that may be relevant for church members. The results of these considerations may then become part of the church's input to broader discussions of such themes that are going on in society. Meanwhile, the General Synod has accepted two such discussion papers for use at all levels of church life and beyond. The first one, which is entitled *We and our Work: Called in God's World*, deals with issues regarding labor and the economy. The second paper presents thoughts about family life and kinship in an individualistic culture; it is called *Kinship as a Gift: Living in a Web of Relationships*.

A Church with others

The Protestant Church in the Netherlands is a united church. As such, it is by far the largest Protestant church in the country. In keeping with its own church order, it is an ecumenical church. In the first place, this is appropriate in relation to other churches that belong to the same Protestant family. The division in this particular family was only partially overcome by the unification process. In light of the present situation in which the Christian faith is a minority option, there is an urgent need to reexamine the divisions that continue to exist within this part of the Body of Christ. Without denying the importance of the issues which caused these divisions, we must confess that when we look back, they may be viewed as being something of a luxury.

Presently, the Roman Catholic Church is not in a very ecumenical mood. In particular, the possibility of intercommunion is severely restricted. Nevertheless, Protestantism needs to engage in ongoing dialogue with the Roman Catholic Church and cannot sit, satisfied, in its own Protestant corner. Protestantism is permanently in danger of becoming "sectarian" – which certainly will be the case if the dialogue with the Roman Catholic Church comes to an end.

In addition to the traditional churches, there are some relative newcomers in the Netherlands, which include Pentecostal and Evangelical churches. In 2008, the PCN decided to start a dialogue with the Pentecostal community. The first results of this discussion are expected in 2014. There is genuine openness to entering into this dialogue on both sides. That is a recent phenomenon; previously, Protestants viewed Pentecostals as being fanatics, whereas Pentecostals saw Protestants as being liberals who kept the Spirit at a distance. Happily, these prejudices are now being questioned.

The phenomenon of migrant churches may be even more important. In fact, for the most part, these churches represent the presence of the South in the North and point to the shift in Christianity's center of gravity from the North to the South. Some of these migrant churches are Roman Catholic congregations, while many others have a Pentecostal identity. These congregations are often quite vital, although for the most part, they do not intermingle with "white" Dutch Christianity. Even so, a considerable part of the witness to the gospel in our country bears the stamp of color. Thus, the Spirit moves in a mysterious way. The PCN will make efforts to establish good relations with these migrant churches, particularly through *Samen Kerk in Nederland* (SKIN; "Together Church in the Netherlands"), which is an association in which many migrant churches participate.

The Council of Churches still plays an important role in the Netherlands, and the PCN is a key player in this Council. However, as with other international ecumenical bodies, the Council seems to have exceeded its capacities. In addition to this Council, a movement called the Dutch Christian Forum has developed. It is a variant of the Global Christian Forum, which seeks to arrange meetings where representatives of all Christian churches and denominations may share faith, encouragement, and the attentiveness needed to respond to the Spirit. Thus, the institution (the Council) and the movement (the Forum) may strengthen each other.

Concluding remarks

Looking back to the vision paper, I will offer this summary:
1. The Protestant Church in the Netherlands wants to be clear about its identity as the Body of Christ and as a community that lives from the gospel of the risen Lord. To live this identity and to share our faith, we need each other.
2. The PCN's rootedness in Christ fosters an openness to experimenting with the form of the church. The basic form is a fellowship that gathers in Christ's name. The concrete way that this fellowship is formed depends on tradition, but also on the time and other circumstances.

3. The church is not an agent for some loftier goal. Church life involves living as a community of brothers and sisters who are called to reconcile themselves with God and one another. We need spirituality, but not in an isolating form of private concern; rather, there needs to be a spirituality of communality.

4. The PCN is called to be a church in company with other churches; to earnestly seek unity with other Reformed churches; and to realize that Christianity in the Netherlands no longer is white.

We do not know what the future of the PCN will be. It is realistic to suppose that the church will be a player on the periphery of society. A church, which used to have a place in the center, will have to rediscover itself in this margin. This church for all people, with a mission to the whole of the nation, will itself be a figure on the margin.

This is a time of crisis. It is good to be honest about that. There has to be space to mourn lost members, lost church buildings, and lost congregations. It is cruel to forbid people to mourn. This is a time for mourning, but beyond that, it is a time to go back to the roots. It is a time of *metanoia*, of confessing our sins, our laziness, our self-sufficiency. Above all, it is a time to open ourselves again to the living Lord. It is a time to find out what it means to be faithful witnesses. A time like this is a time full of opportunities. Thus, after ten years of being the Protestant Church in the Netherlands, we can look to the future with hope and courage.

Abbreviations

NRSV: The Bible, New Revised Standard Version.
PCN: Protestant Church in the Netherlands.

The First Ten Years of the Protestant Church in the Netherlands in Dutch Society

Harm Dane

Ten years of social disquiet

It is an understatement to say that Dutch society has been in a state of confusion during the last ten years. There have been five different governmental administrations in as many elections. Traditional parties, such as the
Christian Democrats and the Labor Party, have jumped up and down in the
polls and in their number of members in parliament, while new right and
left wing political parties have had remarkable success. In a referendum,
the Dutch population, which had been a strong supporter of ongoing European integration since the 1960s, voted against the European Constitution.
The Netherlands – which over the years, had become well known throughout the world for its liberal tradition and tolerant atmosphere – became an
example of anti-Islam propaganda, which climaxed with the provocative
movie *Fitna*. In 2002, a leftist animal liberation activist assassinated Pim
Fortuyn, a newcomer to the political scene, who attacked the long-term
dominance of the Social Democrats in Dutch society. That same year, the
well-known moviemaker and sharp satirist of Islam Theo van Gogh was
murdered in public by a young Dutch man who had converted to Islam.

This disconcerting instability in socio-political relations, which had
been unknown since the Second World War, was part of the worldwide
shift in the balance of power that followed the collapse of the Soviet Union
in 1990. The emergence of new economic powers, such as China, Brazil,
and South Africa, produced uncertainty about Europe's position and future
in the world. Since 2008, the international financial and economic crisis
has reinforced and deepened this uncertainty, which has contributed significantly to a reluctance to support further European integration and has

strengthened the search for national identity. Yet, the financial and economic crisis has also led to political decisions to sharply reduce the national budget, as well as to a rise in unemployment and the collapse of
consumer confidence. In short, we have had ten years of instability and
confusion, and there is little agreement in society about a political strategy
for the future.

At first glance, all of this confusion seems to have had little impact
on the Protestant Church in the Netherlands, which was founded in 2004.
On the contrary, the merger of the Netherlands Reformed Church (NRC),
the Reformed Churches in the Netherlands (RCN), and the Evangelical
Lutheran Church in the Kingdom of the Netherlands (ELC) – following a
process that started in 1960, but was intensified at the level of the national
synods in 1990 – was considered by many people who were involved in this
process to be a new starting point, a burst of new energy, and an occasion
for reconsidering the church's mission in society. The process of unification took a lot of energy and was focused on issues of structure and church
law, which dominated many years of debate and confusion and many meetings and synods. Finally, the confusion came to an end. At all levels of
the church, from local congregations to the national synod, a new climate
broke forth, which enabled people to meet as members of one church in
spite of differences in background, heritage, and spirituality.

Yet, all of the new energy could not hide the fact that the number of
church members kept going down and the amount of money collected from
the members was also decreasing. More and more local congregations had
difficulties keeping their budgets balanced, and could no longer afford a
full-time minister. They often had to close church buildings and merge
with other congregations. In addition, it has become more and more difficult for almost all congregations to find people who are willing to take
responsibility as officebearers. Thus, despite the new energy and awareness of the church's mission, its financial and organizational capabilities
have continued to weaken. Furthermore, the church's position in society
has been marginalized since the 1960s, and this process has not come to an
end. The new secularized political climate has even resulted in a tendency
to reconsider the church-state relationship without much knowledge of the
history and characteristics of this relationship. For example, questions have
been raised in public debate regarding whether financial gifts to the church
should be considered to be gifts for the public good and why they should
reduce income taxes, as had been always quite normal and accepted.

Three divisive issues

A question arises regarding whether there is any connection between the developments that have been outlined here. Has there been any interaction between developments inside and outside of the church? Or has the Protestant Church in the Netherlands become so marginalized – so pushed to the edges of society – that it is useless to search for a common frame of reference in an attempt to understand what is going on and what this means for the church in its devotion to the gospel and its dedication to society? As we enter into this question more deeply, we need to keep in mind the fact that during the years preceding 2004, there was rather strong resistance in the three churches to the proposed unification. With ten years behind us, we can now discern three major topics of debate. The first has to do with the historical roots of the NRC and its national identity as a church that had been rooted in Dutch society since the Reformation (see above, 24). This struggle regarding identity culminated in a debate about the name of the new church. Those who insisted on unbroken continuity between the new church and the church of the Reformation maintained that the name of the new church should look a lot like the name of the RCN. For them, preserving s similar name was an act of obedience to God – who they believed had founded the national church of the Netherlands himself. Thus, for the people who defended the old name, the debate about the name of the new church primarily had to do with national identity.

The second hot topic was of a completely different character; it had to do with the autonomy of local congregations, which was relatively common in the RCN (see above, 25). At the heart of the matter was the question of whether the local congregation was the sole owner of the local church building if it eventually felt a moral duty to leave the denomination out of obedience to the correct understanding of the Word of God. This issue had to do with viewing the church in terms of local congregations that have a responsibility to preserve the true understanding of the Word and will of God and an obligation to leave the national union of local faith communities if that body were to depart from this true understanding. It involved a fear of a hierarchical, "top-down" church and a fear of centralized power, which was another example of the fear of losing one's own identity. In this case, however, the concern was with local identity.

The third debate revolved around the question of the possibility of conducting church weddings for same-sex couples (see above, 18,24). It was hard to find a solution to this issue because there were two strong wings holding opposing views. One group insisted that the church should ac-knowledge its obligation to accept all couples, whether heterosexual or homosexual, who want to have a church wedding. The other wing – with similar conviction – saw this as being a denial of the will of God and re-fused to accept the idea that the church should allow homosexual partners to have their union solemnized by the church. This debate had to do with personal identity, with the relationship between personal autonomy and living as a Christian, and with each individual's personal responsibility to discern God's will for his/her own life.

Thus, we may conclude that the struggle to come together to form the PCN can be characterized as a struggle for identity on three levels – namely, for national identity, local identity, and personal identity. Now the question is whether there is a connection between these struggles for identity within the three churches and the disorientation that has characterized Dutch soci-ety during the last ten years. Is there any relationship between the struggle for identity within the church and the confusion within society?

A typology from the work of Dietrich Bonhoeffer

To investigate this question, I want to use a typology proposed by Diet-rich Bonhoeffer in his dissertation *Sanctorum Communio*, which was com-pleted in 1927 and published in 1930. Having grown up in a family that had wide interest in the social sciences, the young theologian became in-terested in the question of community. From his point of view, European culture had had an insoluble problem ever since the time of the Renais-sance – that is, a tension between the individual and society or between the person and the group. After the Renaissance, European culture could be characterized as an ongoing effort to combine belonging to a group or a nation and being an independent individual. Bonhoeffer distinguished four types of solutions in European culture that sought to bridge this tension between "we" and "I" although all of them eventually proved to be insuf-ficient. His typology of four kinds of "we" – of social constructs designed to cope with the tension mentioned above – is as follows:
– The Aristotelian We is characterized by the dominance of the group's political form. Ultimately, each individual is described as a citizen of the *polis*, which is a group defined by laws and government. As a citizen, each person has the right and opportunity to be an individual.

– The Cartesian We is based on the conviction that all people have been created with the same intelligence and gifted with the same ability to think and act in a reasonable way. This rationality is able to unite people, thus giving them the right and ability to think for themselves and to make their own judgments.
– The Stoic We is characterized by the brotherhood of humankind. This type of We is grounded in the metaphysical unity of human beings. Although each person has his/her own identity, all people belong to each other because they are all human beings. Therefore, they are able to share feelings and emotions of joy and suffering and are able to form groups.
– The Epicurean We is characterized by the drive that each individual has to look out for him/herself. Because everyone watches out for himself by searching for the good life, people are able to work and live together; they need each other to satisfy their individual desires.

As stated above, no type of We "meets the mark." Sooner or later, there will be a repressive type of domination of the group over the individual in types 1 and 2, and in types 3 and 4, there eventually will be a dearth of community because of the concentration on the self. Of course, these types are academic constructs. In reality, a particular group might be characterized by one or two of the aforementioned types, while the non-dominant types slumber below the surface.

On the basis of this typology, Bonhoeffer described European culture as being characterized by a permanent struggle between these four types of We. I think that this typology can help us characterize both Dutch society since the Second World War and the developments that occurred during the process of uniting to form the Protestant Church in the Netherlands. In applying this typology, I will try to account for current tensions between church and society.

A brief sketch of Dutch society after the Second World War

It is possible to characterize Dutch society as providing a good example of the Aristotelian We after the Second World War. Despite sharp differences in ideologies and religions, there was a strong desire to rebuild society together following the disastrous experiences of the war, and there was broad acceptance of a political system having different parties and changing coalitions. However, this Aristotelian We also meant the suppression of individuality. The student revolts of the late 1960s can be understood as a threefold protest against this Aristotelian dominance. As a result of growing wealth and education among the general population, there was a struggle for more personal growth and development, as well as a struggle for the right to make one's own decisions about relationships, sexuality, and lifestyle. Secondly, there was also a struggle to engage in political debate, as critics spoke out against capitalistic structures and the political system and protested against the Vietnam War and the underdevelopment of neocolonial countries. Thirdly, we saw the flower power movement, which insisted on the unity of the human community despite all of the apparent differences, singing "all you need is love." This threefold revolt against Aristotelian dominance in society brought about more than a decade of confusion and creativity, as well as a number of political movements and social initiatives.

Yet, if we jump ahead 20 years, we find that the climate had changed profoundly. The political scene was dominated by an ideology of technical efficiency in governance, accompanied by a strong belief that the market is characterized by rational interactions among various participants who seek to reach fixed goals with the highest results at the lowest prices. This market rationality was covered with a "sauce" made of stoic optimism, in which ideological differences no longer played an important role. During the period between 1994 and 2002, a long-lasting governing coalition was formed between the liberal VVD Party and the social democratic PVDA Party for the first time since 1945. This was also the first time since 1903 that the government did not include members from any of the Christian democratic parties. Everybody insisted on tolerance and personal liberties. The climate in society was characterized by an Epicurean liberalism, which encouraged everyone to look out for him/herself and – in keeping with the Stoic emphasis on everybody being an individual with the right to shape his or her own life in the desired ways – made everybody responsible for his or her own well-being. As we shall see a little later, it is important to highlight the dominance of the Epicurean and Stoic atmosphere in Dutch society during the 1990s.

First, however, we must mention the shock that society felt when, out of the blue, Pim Fortuyn suddenly made a victorious entrance into the political arena. He destroyed the self-satisfied atmosphere that pervaded politics by exposing deep feelings of dissatisfaction among a lot of people. These feelings were the result of anxiety about the growing number of foreign residents in the Netherlands, many of whom were people from Mediter-ranean countries with their own religion and culture. The feelings of dis-satisfaction also represented a protest against the Stoic climate among the in-crowd of politicians, which may be expressed in these terms: "We leave each other totally free to do whatever each one wants."

People felt that their anxieties and confusions about "Dutch identity" were being ignored, and they felt that the hedonistic Epicurean lifestyle to which they had come accustomed during the previous decade was being threatened. Thus, Fortuyn and, following his shocking assassination, Geert Wilders redefined the social climate by insisting on supposedly Western and European values and by speaking about the irrationalities of Islam and the backwardness of people from Arab countries. This was said to be exemplified by their attitude against homosexuality and emphasis on the importance of religion in the public sphere. An important topic of public debate became the necessity for people to become integrated into society by becoming decent citizens according to the more or less evident stan-dards of Dutch citizenship. Fortuyn and Wilders also stressed the impor-tance of restoring law and order to society, because the climate of tolerance had resulted in the feeling that the attitude toward criminals had become much too kind and punishments had become much too lax. Thus, applying Bonhoeffer's typology, we can say that at the beginning of the twenty-first century, there was a massive protest against the dominant Stoic climate in which people felt their Epicurean and Aristotelian sensitivities being threatened.

Three cultures in one church

Incidentally, I agree that using Bonhoeffer's typology does not explain ev-erything about the changes that have taken place in Dutch society. I have not attempted to explore all of the factors that may have resulted in these shifts from one dominant socio-cultural form to another. Jürgen Habermas speaks of an ongoing reorganization of solidarity that has been taking place in European countries since the Middle Ages. Bonhoeffer's typology offers us a tool that may help us describe this reorganization of solidarity. In addi-tion, it gives me an opportunity to relate the changes that have occurred in the Dutch socio-cultural milieu during the last forty years to the dominant cultures of the three merging churches.

Although, in the 1980s, the three churches acknowledged that there were no fundamental theological obstacles to prevent them from working toward a merger, a significant impediment to the process of uniting was posed by the differing socio-cultural atmospheres that characterized the three churches. I will again use the Bonhoeffer typology to describe these differences. The NRC can be described as being dominated by the Aristotelian We. The coherence of that church was based on its institutional form and church law. Everyone in the church agreed that there were deep differences among its constituents with regard to theology, faith, and ethics. The sense of being one church was rooted in the institution of the national church, which had been strongly related to Dutch history and to the Dutch people since the Reformation. In contrast, the culture of the RCN can be characterized as being based on a Cartesian attitude, insofar as the unity of the church was grounded in one faith, one doctrine, and one conviction. Of course, this fact was related to the history of the RCN, which had come into being in the nineteenth century as a result of the conviction shared by those who left the NRC that the denomination was no longer proclaiming the true gospel. With regard to the ELC, we can say that at the end of the twentieth century, it consisted of a mix of the Stoic and Epicurean We's. There was a liberal climate in which everyone was free to disagree without much struggle or debate and in which there was great tolerance for – and acceptance of – each other's personal choices. At the same time, everyone felt united by a sophisticated liturgy and the great attention paid to rituals and music during the worship services.

Although these socio-cultural differences among the three churches were neglected during the unification process, they constitute the background of some of the distinctive differences among the three churches and their members. These differences eventually led to dissimilar methods of making decisions, as well as to divergent attitudes toward ministers and elders, approaches to pastoral care, and understandings of membership. For example, In the NRC, each minister of a local congregation was always a representative of the national church as well; therefore, he (or she, although women pastors were not accepted by the whole church!) represented an authority beyond the local congregation. In the ELC, the minister's authority was based on his/her role as the key person involved in carrying out the liturgy and celebrating the Lord's Supper. In the RCN, authority was based on the minister being a studious theologian, responsible for keeping the congregation in line with the one and only true doctrine, but responsibility for the church as such lay with the elders and the church council at the local level. The people who left the NRC in the nineteenth century had built churches in every community where they could afford to do so; thus, they felt that they were responsible for the church as an institution. People in the NRC used the church as an eternal shelter, which would always be there to comfort them if they needed it, whereas from the very beginning, people in the RCN had been familiar with the idea that they must build the church themselves by being responsible for and active in the life of the local congregation throughout their lifetime. In the ELC, the church was a place to celebrate life.

A clash of cultures

This is not the place to go into further detail about socio-cultural differences among the three churches. My point concerns the mismatch between the cultural climates of the churches and cultural developments in society. As mentioned above, during the 1990s – which were the most intense years of the churches' attempt to find a way to combine the NRC's Aristotelian We and the RCN's cultural legacy, which was based on the Cartesian We – society's cultural milieu was dominated by the Epicurean and the Stoic We. Thus, it may not come as a surprise that both inside and outside of the church, there was a strong lack of interest in the process of uniting. People were looking for experiences and events, spirituality and communication; thus, they were not very interested in structures, rules, church polity, and doctrines. Furthermore, during the ten years of the PCN's existence, a strong tendency to focus on the Aristotelian We of citizenship and national identity has combined with an aversion to and mistrust of institutions, no matter whether these be governmental or private. Yet, there has also been a focus on the Epicurean We by liberal and tolerant people who do not bother themselves with each other's lifestyles or religion as long as others don't bother them – which is to say, as long as everyone behaves in the public sphere in a way that is appropriate in a secularized society.

This mismatch of cultures does not need to be a misfortune for the church. Nevertheless, I think that there is a problem facing the church. The unity of the PCN is based on church law and on the church's existence as an institution. However, being an institution produces very little resonance among the general population or among church members. This gives rise to feelings of alienation from the church as an institution and to a lack of credibility. Let me offer two examples of this, one of which is related to membership and the other which has to do with the position of elders.

The first principle of church order that deals with membership, states that a person's membership in a local congregation is based on where he/she lives, although it is possible to transfer to another congregation. However, in a "liquid society" (to use the term of the sociologist Zygmunt Bauman), membership is not as stable as the institution would like it to be. People often choose the congregation where they feel at home for the time being. Due to biographical factors, it is likely that they will eventually move to another congregation, whether it is part of the PCN or not. More and more people are no longer interested in church boundaries; they go where they like the worship atmosphere and the spirituality, or they choose a congregation with people in a similar age range or with kids that are the same age as their own. This indicates that church members first and foremost see themselves as belonging to a specific congregation, rather than as being members of the nationwide church. In relation to Bonhoeffer's typology, we may say that the question of church membership is increasingly being decided on the basis of an Epicurean attitude, despite the Aristotelian approach to membership that is mandated by the institution.

This is a confusing development for elders serving on the church council. They want to comfort and please the members by providing a good spiritual atmosphere and social climate. However, they are also responsible for finances, the building, and other formal duties. These two types of responsibility are not always in agreement with each other, and they can be in direct conflict in cases where a lack of money necessitates painful decisions. In such situations, we either see church members who are not interested in taking responsibility leaving the congregation or church members challenging the church council and even calling in a lawyer. In both approaches, there is little awareness of the church's existence as the body of Christ. Thus, the elders, who are responsible for the congregation as a legal entity, find themselves in a position between the devil and the deep blue sea.

So far, the church's response to these developments has been rather poor. There has been an official evaluation of church law, without significant debate about that law in relation to the church's position in society. A serious attempt to renew the position of ordained ministers in the face of the church's marginalization by society had been frustrated by a rather stubborn lack of will at the synodal level. This stalemate is based on the argument (which has frequently been repeated for decades) that there is no clarity regarding a theology of ordained and unordained officeholders in the church. This reluctance could be explained as the normal resistance to change which surfaces when people feel insecure about the future, but I think there is a deeper reason that the church is having difficulty relating to the dominant Epicurean culture. That is, the Epicurean view of human beings has never had theological justification or support. It is not difficult to see that the Aristotelian, Cartesian, and Stoic approaches to solidarity have always had theological support and justification. However, the Epicurean standpoint has been treated in a stepmotherly way, and has been seen as representing an inferior moral attitude. This underestimation of the Epicurean We is remarkable in light of the warm support given to the other types of social cohesion, especially when we realize that all four of them are inadequate and, sooner or later, will pose a moral threat to social life, although they all four simultaneously represent an important aspect of that which makes the human person a social being. This is not the place to resolve this issue. For the moment, the point that I want to emphasize is that during its first ten years of existence, the PCN has failed to make contact with the dominant Epicurean culture because of a deeply rooted theological prejudice against this aspect of social life.

New creativity

In this essay, I have pointed to the tension that exists between the church as an institution and the behavior of people in today's society. However, this focus might obscure the fact that there is a lot of energy and creativity in many congregations. Committed church members are aware of the decline in church membership, and a number of them, supported by elders, ordained ministers, and other professionals, are seeking new ways to be the church, new forms of liturgy, and new activities. Those participating on a local level no longer are frustrated by the church's marginalized position in society. There is a lot of energy and creativity, in spite of the painful necessity to decide to sell a church building or to reduce the size of the appointment of a new minister. Difficult decisions will have to be made in the coming years concerning the church's structure and governance, but we know that these mechanisms are mere instruments for the mission of the church, which is the proclamation of the gospel in our country. We may trust that the Holy Spirit will inspire us to find new ways to fulfill the on-

going drive to share the good news with everyone who is willing to hear
it.

Abbreviations and bibliography

ELC: Evangelical Lutheran Church in the Kingdom of the Netherlands.
NRC: Netherlands Reformed Church.
PCN: Protestant Church in the Netherlands.
RCN: Reformed Churches in the Netherlands.

Bauman, Zygmunt. 2005. Liquid life. Cambridge: Polity Press.
Bonhoeffer, Dietrich. 1930. Sanctorum Communio: Eine dogmatische Unter-
    suchung zur Soziologie der Kirche. Edited by Joachim von Soosten. DBW
    1, 1986. München: Kaiser.
Habermas, Jürgen. 2008. Nach dem Bankrott. In: Die Zeit, Jahrgang 2008, Aus-
    gabe 46. Accessed July 11, 2013. http://www.zeit.de/2008/46/Habermas.

Part II

Stories from other Contexts

To Give a Better Witness to the Gospel:
The United Protestant Church of Belgium

Hugh Robert Boudin

A glance backwards

Belgium – or more precisely the Southern Netherlands – was the scene
of the first two martyrdoms of advocates of the Lutheran Reformation of
the sixteenth century. The Augustinian monks Hendrik Voes and Jan van
Esschen from the Antwerp Convent were burned at the stake in Brussels'
Market Square on July 1, 1523. Upon hearing about this event, Martin
Luther wrote a twelve-stanza hymn entitled *Ein neues Lied wir heben an*,
whose first verse reads as follows in English translation:

> *By help of God I fain would tell*
> *A new and wondrous story,*
> *And sing a marvel that befell*
> *To his great praise and glory.*
> *At Brussels in the Netherlands*
> *He hath his banner lifted,*
> *To show his wonders by the hands*
> *Of two youths, highly gifted*
> *With rich and heavenly graces.*

Since this dramatic beginning, indigenous Protestantism has gone through
a chequered history full of executions, battles, and disappearances under-
ground, where it flowed like a subterranean river before reappearing when
the circumstances were more favorable.

In 1566, Catholic and Protestant nobles, who were indignant that their
cherished liberties had been drastically curtailed, formed a League for the
purpose of presenting their claims to Archduchess Isabella, the Governess

of the Southern Netherlands, who held the country in the name of King Philip II of Spain. This Compromise of the Nobles spearheaded the ensuing revolt against Spanish absolutism and gave a name – *Geus* – and a symbol – a double bag suspended from two clasping right hands – to the freedom fighters.

> *Ainsi par le sel, le pain et la besace,*
> *Jamais les Gueux ne changeront quoi que l'on fasse.*
> By this salt, this bread, and this knapsack,
> These Beggars shall never change whatever happens.

Ten years later, the Pacification of Ghent epitomized the hope for an agreement among the different factions of citizens facing political and religious absolutism. However, the fall of Antwerp in 1585 was an important phase in the *Reconquista* by the famous *tercios*, the elite Spanish fighting force in Europe. Nearly two decades later, on September 20, 1604, with banners unfurled, drums beating, and musketwicks alight, Dutch troops marched in formation out of the besieged town of Ostend. Following a direct order from the States-General, the last Protestant bastion of the Southern Netherlands surrendered to the Spanish commander Spinola. The curtain fell on what could have been the finishing blow to Protestantism. However, the few surviving congregations slipped into a clandestine existence and became churches "under the Cross" that survived as well as they could.

In 1648, the Treaty of Münster brought some appeasement to the religious quarrelling, without bringing about full-fledged toleration. Recent research has shown that the Protestant diaspora was far more prevalent than the two frequently-mentioned remnants at Horebeke in East Flanders and Hodimont near Verviers on the Vesdre River. Families that were deprived of pastoral assistance and small groups that did not have any structure were the discreet witnesses to a weakened Protestantism.

Liberty saw a new dawn when Emperor Joseph II signed the Patent of Toleration (*Toleranz Patent*) in 1781. Protestant worship was allowed with the permission of the authorities, although it had to be without ostentation or public display because no spectacle was to be created. Benefiting from the military conquests of the French Revolution, indigenous Protestants saw their legal status improve under the Napoleonic Code. Their emancipation slowly continued under the Dutch regime until the Kingdom of Belgium came into being. The head of this new state was the Lutheran prince

Leopold of Saxe-Coburg-Gotha, under whom Protestants could envisage obtaining full religious liberty.

Looking at the eighteenth century – and taking the period from 1750 to 1814 into account – forty-one Protestant congregations (excluding Anglican parishes) can be identified. In 1814, ten of these were dissolved without any hope of revival; six no longer had a minister; eight were dormant, but could potentially be revitalized; and seventeen led a comparatively normal life. When the United Kingdom of the Netherlands was created at the Congress of Vienna in 1815, the total number of Protestant churches was thirty, although this figure would increase to fifty-six by 1830.

A first partner

When considering church unification in Belgium, one must continually remember that one is dealing with a church that nearly passed into oblivion several times. Indeed, the Belgian Revolution also dispersed existing congregations by disrupting the Presbyterian structure that the Netherlands Reformed Church had given them. However, living under a new regime and the new constitution of 1831, Protestants in Belgium could count on full freedom in matters of doctrine, ethics, and church government, following their foretaste of this between 1815 and 1830 under the benevolent reign of William I, the sovereign of the United Kingdom of the Netherlands.

In 1839, the Synod of the Union of Evangelical Protestant Churches of the Kingdom of Belgium was recognized by the state as the sole Protestant authority in the country. This body had a Congregationalist flavor since it brought together congregations that were quite set on preserving their local autonomy. This Union of Churches was recognized as the official Protestant church in Belgium by the Ministry of Justice, which was responsible for religious affairs. The president of the synod, who was democratically elected by representatives of the local congregations, was considered to be the head of the Belgian Protestant Church and acted as such in all official capacities. He was the link between the authorities and the local churches.

A second partner

A daughter of the revival that swept through Europe during the nineteenth century, the *Société Evangélique Belge* – which ultimately became the *Eglise Réformée de Belgique* – appeared on the Belgian scene in 1837.

A few pastors and laymen of the official Protestant church were eager to evangelize. In the wake of the work that was undertaken in Belgium by the British and Foreign Bible Society, they started small Bible study groups for people who were eager to hear more about the biblical message. Working hand in hand, evangelism and efforts to eliminate illiteracy led to the creation of churches and schools. To call attention to the society's goal, a process of "churchification" took place. This was reflected by a change of name, as the *Société Evangélique Belge* became the *Eglise Chrétienne Missionnaire Belge* (ECMB). Aspiring to reconnect with the sixteenth century, the ECMB adopted the *Confessio Belgica* (Belgic Confession), although it omitted Article 36 (which deals with earthly authorities) since its leadership had resolutely chosen a Free Church stance.

In the Jubilee year of 1887, the ECMB administered thirty-five worship locations with some seven thousand members, who primarily came from the lower social strata. Special ties were maintained with French-speaking Reformed churches in the Swiss Cantons of Vaud, Geneva, and Neuchâtel. Their young pastors found a place to try out their pastoral skills in Belgium. The ECMB's social outreach took the form of an orphanage, retirement homes, cooperatives like groceries and bakeries, and temperance societies. It published many tracts and periodicals, such as *Le Chrétien Belge*, the *Revue Protestante Belge*, and the weekly *Paix et Liberté*. As a Free Church, the ECMB depended on the generosity of its members, supplemented by gifts from other churches in neighboring countries, including Switzerland in particular. In the wake of theological developments, a decision to specify its nature was made in 1970, and the ECMB became the *Eglise Réformée de Belgique – Hervormde Kerk van België.*

A third partner

The history of the Reformed Churches in Belgium (*Gereformeerde Kerken in België*, GKB) began in the Netherlands in the nineteenth century. In reaction to liberal theology, a movement arose which wanted to re-emphasize confessional texts such as the Belgic Confession and the Heidelberg Catechism. This caused a split in the Netherlands Reformed Church, led to the birth of the Reformed (*Gereformeerde*) Churches in the Netherlands (RCN), and had an impact on some families living in Brussels, who left the Belgian church in the capital. On December 20, 1894, the *Gereformeerde* Church of Brussels was founded, followed by the *Gereformeerde* Church of Antwerp in 1899. Both became part of the RCN. Evangelization give rise to the establishment of similar churches in Ghent in 1926, in Mechelen in 1938, and in Denderleeuw, Antwerp-Hoboken, and Boechout in 1953. The membership of these six churches – which were served by eight pastors – amounted to two thousand individuals. In 1927, the Synod of the RCN set up a Committee for Evangelism in Belgium. Offshoots of this work included Protestant primary schools and the publication of a periodical entitled *De Open Poort*. According to the church order, every RCN congregation had to be part of a classis. The Classis Dordrecht began to host the Belgian congregations in 1896.

In 1951, the *Kring België* was started, making contacts with other churches in Belgium much easier. The RCN's congregations in Belgium were becoming integrated into the local and national context. They participated actively in the work of the commissions of the Federation of Protestant Churches in Belgium, such as those which dealt with the Third World, youth work, and radio and television. They were also involved in the Belgian Missionary Department (*Département Missionaire Belge*), the Belgian Bible Society, the Protestant Theological Faculty of Brussels, and Protestant religious education. The desire to cooperate more fully with the Protestant Evangelical Church of Belgium (*Eglise Protestante Evangélique de Belgique* – *De Protestants-Evangelische Kerk van België*; EPEB-PEKB) prompted the GKB – with the explicit permission of its Synod – to accept subsidies from the Belgian government. In 1968, the two partners signed a covenant. In the meantime, a *Classis België* was created. This new structure ensured smoother cooperation. On April 8, 1978, the General Synod of the RCN approved the GKB's participation in discussions regarding the formation of the United Protestant Church of Belgium (UPCB). The Committee for Belgian Affairs was given the responsibility of accompanying the GKB through that entire process and of caring for future relationships between the RCN and the UPCB. In the hope of creating a renewed church, the GKB participated eagerly in all of the discussions leading up to the unification of the historically Protestant churches in Belgium.

Moving towards unity: a slow process

The maturation of the process of moving towards unity took a number of years, and several phases can be identified prior to the formation of the

UPCB. In 1844, the Synod of the Union of Evangelical Protestant Churches created a commission to provide pastoral care to Protestants who were part of the diaspora and to serve citizens who were on a spiritual quest. In 1880, *Stads- en Landsevangelisatie Silo* founded several congregations in Flanders. In 1922 – following the First World War – the German-speaking churches in Eupen, Neu-Moresnet, Malmédy, and Sankt-Vith joined the Belgian Synod. In 1957 – spurred by a surge of theological renewal – the Union transformed itself into the Protestant Evangelical Church of Belgium (*Eglise Protestante Evangélique de Belgique – De Protestants-Evangelische Kerk van België*) with which the Silo congregations merged. The after effects of the Great War on church life gave rise to twenty new faith communities founded by the Methodist Church. In 1969 – after five years of discussions – the EPEB-PEKB and the Methodist churches formed a new entity called the Protestant Church of Belgium (*Eglise Protestante de Belgique – De Protestantse Kerk van België*; EPB-PKB). To mark this first important step on the road to the Protestant church's unity in Belgium, a royal audience was granted to the new synod president, Dr. A. J. Pieters. At that time, he gave King Bedouin a gold replica of the *Geuzenpenning* (Beggars' Medal) bearing the appropriate motto *"Fidèles au roi jusques à porter la besace."* (Faithful to the King, even to carrying the beggars' bag.) The next phase of the unification process was to be implemented by holding trilateral debates between the EPB-PKB, the *Eglise Réformée de Belgique – Hervormde Kerk van België*, and the *Gereformeerde Kerken Kring België*. Church unity was progressing once again, and led to the birth of the UPCB in 1978.

Speaking in terms of the primary languages spoken in different regions of Belgium, the uniting churches may be categorized in the following way: The Protestant Church of Belgium had French, Dutch, and German-speaking congregations, which utilized the three official languages of the country. In addition, one Hungarian-speaking and two English-speaking churches were members. The *Eglise Réformée de Belgique* had forty French-speaking congregations and three Dutch churches. The GKB had only Dutch-speaking churches. Yet, they all blended into one and the same church: the UPCB.

Flexibility in the unification process

Structural unity was thus achieved among these three bodies, but the scope of the Protestant witness in Belgium was larger. A solution was found for groups that were outside the new fold, but felt a desire to draw closer to it. With a remarkable sense of flexibility, the UPCB's constitution anticipated their needs and offered various options for cooperation. The status of 'partner churches' accommodates those churches that have their own structure and organization, but nevertheless wish to enter into a closer form of living together. The Salvation Army, Baptists, Seventh Day Adventists, and Free Methodists are partner churches. Meetings are held periodically to discuss common problems and establish general policies on a national level. This type of sharing had not taken place previously, but new forms of working together are now being discovered.

Another form of living together has also been set up: the 'affiliated church'. This option is designed for churches that are eager to enter into a closer fellowship, but cannot join the UPCB as full members for a legitimate reason. For example, the *Eglise Protestante Française de Cantorbéry* in England falls into this category because it lives outside Belgium, at the other side of the Channel. Other instances of this situation include the *Deutschsprachige Gemeinde*, Belgian Lutheran churches, and Korean churches. A third form of connection is the 'administrative agreement'. Here, the UPCB helps various church groups negotiate their relationships with Belgian authorities and offers advice regarding church-related matters.

The UPCB's appearance on the ecclesiastical scene in Belgium has set in motion a number of centripetal forces leading to a pan-Protestant striving. Its leaders have sensed this receptiveness and have tried to offer forms of cooperation that respond to these needs and longings to get to know one another. This development has ended the "splendid isolation" in which denominations used to live. We are not aware that this kind of cooperation of satellite communities centered around a united church has been inaugurated in the Netherlands or in other countries, for that matter.

With regard to chronology, it is not without a certain sense of satisfaction, tinged with a little pride, that we recall that the formation of the UPCB occurred in 1978, whereas the founding of the *Protestantse Kerk in Nederland* dates from May 1, 2004 and the establishment of the *Eglise Protestante unie de France* was approved in 2013. Wedged in between these two neighbors, Belgian Protestantism achieved unity at an earlier date. Because of their size, minority churches can proceed at a faster pace than big ecclesiastical organizations consisting of a large number of parishes and elaborate structures. Small is not only beautiful; it can also be very efficient.

Unity and paradox

The history of the merger of Protestant churches in Belgium has the merit of disclosing a paradoxical situation. Persecution, the Inquisition, and state power combined to make the ecclesiastical consequence of the Reformation a religious minority. Given this unfavorable statistical position, one would expect that in the presence of a powerful common adversary, small congregations would try to find security by pooling their resources and endeavoring to join forces. However, this happened only after a period of mistrust and lack of confidence in each other had been resolved. The issues posed by "free churchmanship" – which insisted on having no relationship whatsoever with any state entity, especially in cases that involved financial assistance – stymied all inclinations toward merging with congregations that did accept state money. Fear of state control and oversight, which would try to use the church as an ally in order to further certain political aims, nourished the resolve of the Free Church *"libristes"* to persevere in their conviction that the church must be truly "independent." A somewhat schizophrenic attitude was to be found among the Swiss pastors who performed their "Foreign Legion" pastoral apprenticeship in Belgium. They supported their parishioners in maintaining a Free Church policy, but when their stay in Belgium ended, they went back to their home cantons where their churches were official state churches.

In contrast, the *Union des Eglises* was not eager to leave the "fleshpots" of state subsidies or to abandon the official status which their legal recognition had granted them. The issue of the relationship between church and state was detrimental to efforts to achieve an organizational union. Promoters of both the official church and the Free Church were convinced that their side represented the true Protestant point of view, and they assigned great importance to their duty to defend that position.

Common destiny

Out of all of the European churches, Belgian Protestant congregations are the ones that have had the privilege of sharing in the destiny of Dutch Protestantism throughout the centuries. From the time of the Reformation onwards, when the Low Countries took the political form of the Seventeen Provinces, Protestants in that region were in synodical unity and confessional harmony through the common Belgic Confession. Later, when the separation between the Spanish Netherlands and the United Provinces became an irreversible fact, the churches in the South could still count on assistance from the North, which sent travelling ministers and engaged in retaliation for the *Paepsche stoutigheden (Papal wickednesses)* that their fellow Protestants underwent at the hands of the Spanish regime. The mere existence of Walloon congregations (see above, 11) in the Netherlands prior to the influx of the Huguenots provides a venerable example of this common fate.

Comparing notes

In 2009, i.e. five years after its birth, the Protestant Church in the Netherlands (PCN) felt the need for an evaluation. In 1992, at the occasion of the celebration of the 150th anniversary of the first Belgian National Synod, the Protestant Theological Faculty in Brussels gave a gift to the church in the form of a *Mémorial Synodal – Synodaal Gedenkboek*. This volume contained a contribution from each of the churches that make up the synod – which, among other things, included details about its constituency, its pastoral role, a plotted history of the congregation, a copy of its periodical, an inventory of the artistic and historical items in its possession, and an explicit statement of its plans for future outreach. This helped the consistories project tentative plans for the coming years and gave them a helpful reminder of what they had decided and a way to monitor feedback.

In the run up to the successful merger, a considerable amount of discussion had gone on in committees and commissions, each of which was given a specific topic to explore. However, participating church members knew perfectly well that all of their efforts had not been the decisive factor. It was the Spirit of the living God which had smoothed over apparently insurmountable difficulties; had overcome legal and financial hurdles; and had implanted in the minds of the participants a willingness to move toward the goal of accepting church unity as a gift from God. The coalescing of kindred minds and their coming together in a fraternal atmosphere void of power struggles and denominational prejudices astonished more than one person and put to shame those who had decided, once and for all, that the whole enterprise was doomed to failure.

Aspects of coming together

The PCN produced a vision paper entitled *Learning to live out of wonder*, which was a short, inspiring text, although it was not a confession of faith. Aware that throughout the course of its history – and especially when profound theological crises were threatening its unity – the Church had often attempted to reframe the tenets of its faith by drafting new confessions of faith. The commission dealing with the faith of the future UPCB pondered this vital matter. It was decided that no new formulation of faith was necessary. Picking up on the history of Protestant life and practice in the Netherlands and recognizing the legacy of the Church Universal, a "Declaration of unity and faith" was deemed to be sufficient. However, the wealth of the Church's confessional expressions certainly was not scornfully rejected. On the contrary, when the *Libri Symbolici* of the UPCB was published in a quadrilingual volume, it contained the Apostles' Creed, the Nicean-Constantinopolean and Athanasian Creeds, the Augsburg Confession, the *Confessio Belgica*, the Heidelberg Catechism, and the Articles of Religion. By adopting this multifaceted confessional foundation, the UPCB made clear that it recognized and attached great value to the coming together of an Early Christian-Lutheran-Reformed-Methodist tradition. A peevish mind might take pleasure in noting that bringing together this rainbow of confessional texts meant that contradictions could be found at some points. Nevertheless, the UPCB was ready to embrace this historical reality.

One of the spin-offs of the merger was the real possibility of engaging in prudent church management. Options placed before the new church included streamlining the administration, redistributing the ministries, updating the operations, and simplifying the structures. These alternatives had to take account of vested interests which existed, and legal strategies had to be found so that properties, pension funds, and endowments could be dealt with in ways which recognized that the church is not a commercial enterprise, but a faith community. Satisfactory solutions were eventually discovered.

In *The Heartbeat of Life* of the PCN, Arjan Plaisier says that "the diaconia is a vital part of the church's identity" (see above, 45). The UPCB certainly concurs. With the shifting of society's needs, new institutions have been called into being. Orphanages have been closed, and legal services for asylum seekers have been set up. Debt mediation offices have been opened, and warehouses are offering secondhand furniture. Language courses are helping with integration. Political refugees are being assisted. Exploited girls are being housed, and lodging is being provided for foreign students. The diaconia is becoming a very exacting and specialized undertaking.

What church do we want for the future?

From its inception, the PCN dealt with the question of what kind of church it was and wanted to be. What vision did it have of itself? This same question arose when the UPCB looked at the attitude that it would adopt toward the future. What guidelines would enable the new body's life and practice to be implemented?

First of all, there should be a consciousness of being the part of Christ's Church that was planted in Belgium, is embedded in that country's history, and is especially ready to pursue the task of witnessing within its social setting. Its members should also be aware that being the spiritual descendants of the religious *Geuzen* of the sixteenth century may provide them with a sense of continuity and permanence that is rather unusual in a country like Belgium.

The desire to impart a renewed sense of missionary zeal could easily constitute a trap which careful thinking should seek to avoid. Indeed, old-fashioned evangelism too often turns into an improper eagerness to convert *à tout prix* as – from the height of spiritual arrogance – others' convictions are minimized or even condemned without any serious examination. Instead, having the patience to listen to another person and to make a sustained effort to try to understand him/her must be present in any exploratory mission enterprise that wants to meet real needs and respond to personal queries. Deep convictions do not preclude having an open mind and a desire to share in genuine exchange. Too often minority churches tend to look inwards; thus, they may become a club for initiates and turn into a Christian ghetto. Now we have a novel opportunity to open the windows and doors and to let fresh winds renew the atmosphere, which may have grown rather stuffy.

Ideally the new church should dare to take the risk of carrying out a prophetic interpretation of the modern world and should not seek to accumulate any kind of power, which would be ridiculous anyway, given its minority position. Being a church for others with a deliberate mind of service is a sign of Protestant faithfulness, a mark of evangelical simplicity, and a token of Christian hope.

The openness of the new church, which was a factor in its coming together, smoothed over the rigid identities that had dogged the different partners. One could see signs of real dynamism. The Leuenberg Agreement of 1973 helped create a spirit of reunion, which had a significant impact. The UPCB is, in fact, a reconstituted family, whose different members have come together around two major themes: the unconditional and saving love of God and the church's presence in today's society. In the new church, theological diversity has been received in a positive way. This union is not characterized by uniformity, nor is it merger by absorption.

The challenge of a central position

The UPCB has viewed its duty to function as a bridge between two prominent groups in the modern society of present-day Belgium quite modestly. For three centuries, the clericals and anticlericals have been at each other's throats, but by virtue of its nature the Protestant Church is in a position to extend a hand to these two adversaries. To Roman Catholic-minded citizens – who are not only faithful to their church, but also live in a whole plethora of Catholic social institutions, hospitals, schools, universities, trade unions, publications, and press – the UPCB could emphasize the Christian fellowship that it shares with them by virtue of the fact that they are united through the same Lord. Yet, the UPCB could also remind them that freedom is a prerequisite of an active conscience; that dogmatic pronouncements do not come from the gospel; and that absolutistic church government is akin to dictatorship. Conversely, the "laïque" wing can count on Protestant sympathy and solidarity when it comes to defending human rights; preventing the imposition of one-sided decisions concerning ethical matters on the whole population; and denouncing cover-ups of priest misconduct designed to protect the good name of the Roman Catholic Church. However, the UPCB maintains that a nihilistic attitude which denies God leads nowhere and ends in total hopelessness. It challenges agnostic citizens to study the impact of faith on society and invites them to peruse biblical literature by submitting it to a free examination (*Libre examen*) that lets each individual to decide for him/herself. In both cases, fundamental options for dialogue are shared, but unfortunate deviations from the faith are also exposed. This is a perilous, but worthwhile course of action that reveals the true nature of Protestantism.

An additional benefit of the UPCB's unity must be mentioned. In Belgium's present political situation, there is a tendency for the two main language groups to drift apart and to know less and less about each other. This is a sad development. A selfish, inward-looking attitude, which leads to efforts to grab advantages for one's own group, is commonplace. Regional structures that recognize the rights of all have been established, but the unity of the national synod – which remains a single unit supervising the whole Church body – is maintained. In the Belgian context, this is also an aspect of the church's unity which has significant value as an aspect of the church's witness. The church takes the existence of others into account and bans any narrow-mindedness that is focused exclusively on one's own cultural community.

Conclusion

One could ask why this unification happened. Why establish a united church? What drove the delegates of the participating churches to adopt the unification plan? Was it the spirit of the times that guided them? One of the most important tendencies of our time is the urge to seek the unification or integration of all kinds of movements and organizations. This is true in industry as well as in politics. Was the Belgian churches' decision to merge prompted by a simple desire for unity for unity's sake? Did the churches merely want to do as everyone else was doing? Or was the decision to unite the expression of a hunger for power? Was the small Protestant minority in Belgium intent on forming a united front, so that it could come out of the shadows and exert pressure on the religious, social, economic, and political life of the country? The answer to both series of questions is an emphatic "no." The quest for unity that led to the creation of the new church was prompted solely by the desire to give a better witness to the gospel of our Lord. In other words, the church did not unite in order to be stronger; it united so that it could more effectively serve its contemporaries by proclaiming the Good News of God's love and forgiveness to them by and assuring them of his presence among us.

Abbreviations and bibliography

ECMB:	Eglise Chrétienne Missionnaire Belge (Belgian Christian Mission Church).
EPB-PKB:	Eglise Protestante de Belgique – De Protestantse Kerk van België (Protestant Church of Belgium).
EPEB-PEKB:	Eglise Protestante Evangélique de Belgique – De Protestants-Evangelische Kerk van België (Protestant Evangelical Church of Belgium).
GKB:	Gereformeerde Kerken in België (Reformed Churches in Belgium).
PCN:	Protestant Church in the Netherlands.
RCN:	Reformed Churches in the Netherlands.
UPCB:	United Protestant Church of Belgium.

Boudin, Hugh Robert. 1985. Œcuménisme: L'Eglise Protestante Unie de Belgique. In: La foi et le temps: Revue des diocèses francophones de Belgique, I, janvier–février 1985, XVI, 47–61.

Boudin, Hugh Robert, and Marjan Blok. 1992. Synodaal Gedenkboek van de Verenigde Protestantse Kerk in België – Mémorial synodal de l'Eglise Protestante Unie de Belgique 1839–1992. Brussel: Prodoc.

Boudin, Hugh Robert. 2014 (forthcoming). Alibis de l'Unité du Protestantisme Belge. In: Dictionnaire Historique du Protestantisme et de l'Anglicanisme en Belgique du XVIe siècle jusqu'à nos jours. Joint publication, Brussels: Prodoc – MéMograMes.

Paix & Liberté, numéro spécial, n° 11, 1978.

Pieters, André J., and Emile M. Braekman. 1969. Un événement historique en 1969. In: Bulletin van de Vereniging voor de Geschiedenis van het Belgisch Protestantisme, reeks V, Aflevering 5, 1969/2, 145–150.

De Stem van de Protestantse Kerk en van de Gereformeerde Kerken in België, 107e jaargang, Nr 10, 3 november 1978.

Verenigde Protestantse Kerk in België. In: Centraal Weekblad voor de Gereformeerde Kerken in Nederland, 8 december 1982, 30e jaargang, nr 49.

The Freedom of the Spirit: The United Reformed Church in the United Kingdom

David M. Thompson

The United Reformed Church (URC) was formed in 1972 from the Presbyterian Church of England and a majority of the congregations in the Congregational Church of England and Wales. The new denomination was enlarged in 1981 with the addition of the Re-formed Association of Churches of Christ in Great Britain and Ireland and was expanded even further in 2000 with the inclusion of a majority of the congregations in the Congregational Union of Scotland. In 1973, the first set of church statistics showed that the URC had 2,080 congregations and 192,136 members. The merger in 1981 added 40 churches and 2,317 members, and that of 2000 involved another 51 churches and 4,240 members. Thus, even at its beginning, the URC was one of the smaller Free Churches in the United Kingdom. The Methodist Church was the largest Free Church, and the Baptists were next by a few thousand. However, the established Church of England, the Church of Scotland, and the Roman Catholic Church were significantly larger than any of the Free Church denominations.

The Presbyterians, Congregationalists, and Baptists were the three denominations that emerged from the Dissenters who left the Church of England in 1662 in protest against the Act of Uniformity which was adopted that year. From the beginning, the Presbyterians, who were the most numerous in 1662, and the Congregationalists had much in common and, in fact, had come together briefly in 1691. However, they differed in their understandings of the location of the ultimate authority in the church. The Presbyterians believed that on the local level, this lay with the minister and elders of the local congregation, and beyond that setting, it lay with the

councils of the larger church. In contrast, the Congregationalists believed
that such authority lay with the local congregation's church meeting and
had no broader councils with authority, which was a position shared by
the Baptists, who nevertheless differed with the Congregationalists over
the practice of infant baptism. Yet, organization beyond the local church
was problematic for all dissenters. They were not legally tolerated until
1688, and more comprehensive national organization had to wait until the
nineteenth century. Even then, all of the Dissenters were keenly aware of
their minority status within the country; *political* equality was secured in
the nineteenth century, but any kind of *social* equality had to wait until the
twentieth century.

How it started

Early in the twentieth century, cooperation at the local level gained strength
among the Free Churches, principally to avoid local competition in church-
building. An initiative taken by Congregational churches in the U.S.A. to
interest British Free Churches in the vision of church unity that was inspired by the Edinburgh Missionary Conference of 1910 was another factor
in getting some church leaders excited about the idea of unity. This kind of
cooperation became a reality during the First World War, as the churches
were drawn together to provide chaplains for the troops that were fighting
in France and Belgium. The enthusiasm for Free Church unity on the part
of the Baptist leader J.H. Shakespeare led to the formation of the Federal
Council of Free Churches in 1919. The Lambeth Conference of 1920 pursued the idea of unity, partly at the request of the Episcopal Church in the
USA and partly in pursuit of what was called "home reunion" – which had
been on its agenda since the 1890s. A series of conversations took place
between church leaders from 1920 to 1925, but in the end, these failed
because of the Church of England's insistence on episcopal ordination –
which was one of the issues that had provoked the division in 1662.

Between the wars, the Presbyterian Church of England was involved in
discussions with the Church of Scotland, the Church of England, and the
Episcopal Church of Scotland, as well as with Congregationalists and Baptists in England. After the Second World War, it became clear that the Baptists were not prepared to join any union, except on terms that guaranteed
the independence of local congregations. Therefore, the Congregationalists turned more toward the Presbyterian Church of England, and in 1951,

the first series of conversations resulted in a Covenant to cooperate in all possible ways. When conversations between the Anglicans and the Presbyterians broke down in 1957, it was clear that the only immediate option for church union involved a renewal of conversations between the Presbyterian Church of England and the Congregationalists. The covenant of 1951 had been more fruitful than many had expected, and formal conversations were renewed in 1963. *A Statement of Convictions* was published, and following the British Council of Churches' Faith and Order Conference at Nottingham in 1964, the Churches of Christ accepted an invitation to send three observers to the Joint Committee of Presbyterian and Congregational representatives.

This step was bold for all sides. The problematic issues for the Presbyterians and the Congregationalists primarily had to do with church governance. Although a small group, the Churches of Christ represented a rather different strand in nineteenth-century church life since they practiced the weekly observance of the Lord's Supper and did not accept infant baptism. Yet, they were firmly committed to recovering the unity of the Church. Their congregations were legally independent of one another. However, they had an Annual Conference that had a strong moral authority, even though its decisions could not bind local churches. Moreover, since their ministers were placed with congregations by a conference committee, the churches were accustomed to a closer relationship with the "center" than was the case among the Congregationalists. This meant that involving the Churches of Christ in the conversations between the Congregationalists and the Presbyterians was potentially to complicate them.

The observers from the Churches of Christ made it clear that they did not wish to hold up progress between the two larger churches. Rather, they sought to ensure that the scheme of union for the new church was framed in a way that would make it easier for them to join at a later date. Their success in achieving this meant that the Congregationalists and Presbyterians urged the Churches of Christ to become full partners from the beginning. The observers declined because they (realistically) felt that their congregations needed to be better prepared for the implications of becoming part of the larger church. They organized a program of systematic visits to every congregation in order to secure their support. These could not be completed before the planned date of inauguration, but the Churches of Christ welcomed an invitation to begin formal negotiations at the inaugural Assembly of the United Reformed Church.

Structure

How was the unification of the URC achieved? In effect, the structure of the new church was Presbyterian with a series of councils that did have ultimate authority over the local congregations. Despite Congregational-ism's formal position regarding the independence of the local congrega-tion, that had been significantly modified in practice in the later nineteenth and twentieth centuries. Large urban congregations were still able to have an independent existence if they wished, calling and paying their own min-isters and deciding on their own mission priorities. However, rural con-gregations, which had been the backbone of eighteenth- and nineteenth-century Congregationalism, were significantly weakened by the agricul-tural depression of the later part of the nineteenth century. The number of independent farmers owning their own land – who had often been the principal supporters of rural congregations, standing out against the influ-ence of local gentry and aristocrats – was significantly reduced. As a result, these rural congregations came to depend more on the support of their lo-cal County Unions, which became the chief agents of mission. The rural churches could not afford to pay the higher stipends that urban ministers earned. As the need for a pension program for retired ministers became more pressing at the end of the nineteenth century, this expense was be-yond the capability of all but the largest congregations. Moreover, in the context of the gradual numerical decline that had begun before the First World War but accelerated after it, most Congregationalists' readiness to accept a more structured form of governance beyond the local congrega-tion and the County Union is understandable.

Nevertheless, there were still some ministers and congregations who remained suspicious of what they perceived to be "centralizing" trends in the way Congregationalism was organized in the first half of the twentieth century. There were also some people with a more conservative evangelical theological disposition who were suspicious of what they regarded as a liberal Protestant theology, which they judged to be increasing in influence. Whether that was actually so remains a matter for debate, but these two factions became the basis of the two largest groups of people who voted against the union proposals – although their numbers were insufficient to block the two-thirds majority required for the proposals to be approved.

Since the URC was much larger than its constituent parts, it was de-cided very early on that the practice, which was common to both churches, of allowing every local church to be represented at the Annual Assembly, would be abandoned. Also, it would be necessary to add a larger council between the Presbytery or County Union and the Annual Assembly. The concept of the synod was borrowed from the Church of Scotland (although this alignment had not been very effective there). England and Wales were divided into twelve provinces, each with a synod, presided over by a moderator. The moderator's job primarily involved looking after the itineration of ministers between congregations; he was not really responsible for general oversight of the synod; that was in the hands of the District Councils. The office of Moderator had been taken over from the old Congregational Union, where that person had been responsible for several County Unions, although the number of areas of responsibility was increased. As a result, it was possible for every church to be represented at District Council (which replaced the Presbytery or County Union) and at synod, whereas the members of General Assembly were nominated by District Councils.

Every local congregation had an elders' meeting, as well as a church meeting. Although elders were regarded by some Congregationalists as being an innovation, Congregationalism had, in fact, originally had elders who shared pastoral responsibilities with the minister. However, after the eighteenth century, those elders gradually ceased to be appointed, possibly as a result of the new type of dominance that preaching ministries exerted as a result of the Evangelical Revival. This change left only deacons' meetings, which were more concerned with the congregation's financial affairs. To address the Congregationalists' concern about elders serving for life, it was agreed that in the future, they would serve for limited periods, while remaining eligible for re-election. The Presbyterian practice of ordaining elders, which originally had also been a Congregational practice, was retained.

Theological basis

The theological foundation of the new church was not based directly on either the Presbyterians' Westminster Confession of 1646 or the Independents' Savoy Declaration of 1658, even though there were few differences in the wording of these two statements. The differences that did exist concerned church order and the magistrate's role in the church. Along with the Apostles' and Nicene Creeds, the Westminster Confession and the Savoy Declaration have remained part of the distinctive theological heritage that is acknowledged by the church. The new Basis of Union (BU) was largely based on an intertwining of relevant sentences from the Statement of Faith of the Presbyterian Church of England written in 1956 and the Declaration of Faith adopted by the Congregational Church in 1967. (Those two statements were also regarded as being part of the church's theological heritage.) The special declarations that had to be made by the church's members, elders, and ministers were put into a standard form, and an important Statement on the Nature, Faith, and Order of the United Reformed Church was adopted, with the stipulation that it be read at every service for the ordination or induction of elders and ministers. A key paragraph in this statement declares that "the Lord Jesus Christ, the only ruler and head of the Church, has therein appointed a government distinct from civil government and in things spiritual not subordinate thereto." This assertion picks up on the principle of the separation of civil and spiritual government inherited from English Congregationalism and on the same principle which distinguished the churches that formed the Presbyterian Church in England after the Disruption of the Church of Scotland in 1843.

The churches' common understanding of the Lord's Supper was expressed succinctly in two sentences, which read as follows:

When in obedience to the Lord's command his people show forth his sacrifice on the cross by the bread broken and the wine outpoured for them to eat and drink he himself, risen and ascended, is present and gives himself to them for their spiritual nourishment and growth in grace. United with him and the whole Church on earth and in heaven, his people gathered at his table present their sacrifice of thanksgiving and renew the offering of themselves, and rejoice in the promise of his coming in glory (BU, § 15).

These sentences were based on paragraph 5.10 of the Presbyterian Statement of 1956, which have been nuanced by phrases from paragraph 5.8 of the Congregational Declaration of 1967.

Baptism

Even in 1972, the paragraph on baptism was the longest in the Basis of Union (see BU, § 14). This was the first attempt to express a position that would be acceptable to both those who performed the rite of baptism only following a personal profession of faith by the candidate and those who also practiced infant baptism. One of the first problems that had to be faced involved the fact that there were said to be Congregationalist church members who had never been baptized. This situation was consistent with the seventeenth-century belief that it was one's profession of faith, rather than baptism with water, that made someone a church member. Thus, baptism was described as "the sacrament of entry into the Church" (BU, § 14), rather than as "the means of entry," as an early draft of the Basis of Union had put it.

The paragraph continued with a statement that could be affirmed about baptism at any age: "It makes explicit at a particular time and place and for a particular person what God has accomplished in Christ for the whole creation and for all mankind – the forgiveness of sins, the sanctifying power of the Holy Spirit and newness of life in the family of God" (BU, § 14). The church's involvement in this act was both an affirmation of faith in the action of God in Christ and an assumption of corporate responsibility for those receiving baptism, as the congregation promised to support and nourish them as it received them into its fellowship. This order both affirms the primacy of God's action in baptism and articulates the church's corporate responsibility; thus, baptism cannot be understood as only being a personal affirmation of faith.

The paragraph then stated that baptism could be administered in infancy or at an age of responsibility, and the implications of each type of baptism were specified. This discussion pointed to the idea that baptism entailed a complete process of Christian initiation – without using such an unfamiliar word. In either case, baptism was administered only once to any person. This way of putting the point implicitly acknowledged that neither practice was the norm. Even in 1972, this was a significant step, which had important implications for the long-standing position maintained by united Congregational and Baptist churches where the practical solution to issues associated with baptism was often to follow the practice of the minister's convictions, even if this involved what paedobaptists would regard as rebaptism.

This situation led to the addition of a general paragraph on "the rights of personal conviction" in the church.

The United Reformed Church, believing that it is through the freedom of the Spirit that Jesus Christ holds his people in the fellowship of the One Body, shall uphold the rights of personal conviction. It shall be for the Church, in safeguarding the substance of the faith and maintaining the unity of the fellowship, to determine when these rights are asserted to the injury of its unity and peace (BU, § 10).

This was a significant elaboration of a brief reference to the church's duty to preserve liberty of conscience in paragraph 5.7 of the Congregational Declaration of 1967, insofar as the paragraph in question included a new statement regarding the rights of the *church* in cases where personal convictions were "asserted to the injury of its unity and peace."

   When the negotiations with the Churches of Christ took place later, it became apparent that although their observers had been content with the original statement that they had helped draft, it did not fully state the nature of the issue. Thus, another paragraph was added to expound on this. First, it noted the existence of two different *convictions* about the practice of baptism, which not only involved a difference in the *age* at which baptism was administered (as could be true in any church). This was followed by the affirmation that both convictions were honored by the church. Then, the pastoral consequences of this matter were described:

Should these differences of conviction within the one Church result in personal conflict of conscience it will require to be pastorally reconciled in mutual understanding and charity, and in accordance with the Basis of Union, in the first instance by the Elders' Meeting of the local congregation, and if necessary by the wider councils of the Church (BU, § 14).

The reference to the Basis of Union was designed to point out that this document had already affirmed that baptism was to be administered only once to any person; thus "rebaptism" was ruled out as a solution. A final addition followed:

No one shall be required to administer a form or mode of baptism to which he has a conscientious objection, nor shall the form or mode of baptism used in any instance be one to which conscientious objection is taken by the person seeking baptism or by parent(s) requesting baptism for an infant (BU, § 14).

This statement was meant to cover conscientious scruples by both ministers and candidates, but ministerial scruples were not to prevent baptism taking place in the candidate's local congregation.

   Although some people in the Churches of Christ wanted to retain the possibility of conducting a second baptism, most agreed that this was inconsistent with the practice of the Church throughout the ages. Nevertheless, this tension meant that the final vote in the Churches of Christ was not unanimous, and the two groups agreed to follow their separate ways. Still, there is little doubt that this paragraph has been of great advantage to the URC. It has enabled many persons who had previously been hesitant about infant baptism for their children to follow a path of thanksgiving for child-birth and to seek baptism later. It also made it easier for some Baptists, both ordained and lay, to join the URC as it became clearer that there generally was no interest among Baptists in taking further steps toward church unity.

Communion

The Churches of Christ were less successful in persuading the majority to adopt the practice of weekly Communion. For some Presbyterians, the union of 1972 had represented a change from a quarterly celebration of the Lord's Supper to a monthly communion service. On the other side of the equation, elders of the Churches of Christ who had been ordained to pre-side at Communion were accepted (if they wished) as non-stipendiary min-isters at the time of the union. This became a major stimulus to the intro-duction of non-stipendiary ministry within the URC. However, the empha-sis on college- or course-based training discouraged new recruits for that ministry within the former Churches of Christ. This situation resulted in a shortage of ministers authorized to preside at Communion, which, in turn, reduced the likelihood of the implementation of weekly Communion. The District Councils made provisions for the authorization of non-ministers, usually elders or lay preachers, to preside at celebrations of Communion, but only "in cases of pastoral necessity."

Imbalances

This state of affairs exposed another, less noticed feature of the URC. The geographical spread of the constituent churches was uneven. For exam-ple, apart from Northumberland, there were very few rural Presbyterian churches, whereas there were many rural Congregational churches. Thus, although the new Church embodied an essentially Presbyterian structure of church government, it was largely run by ex-Congregationalists. This has meant, for example, that although the District Council – following appro-priate consultation – has the authority to close local congregations (which was a power that presbyteries had exercised from time to time), this power has very rarely been used within the URC. Similarly, although many of the

Congregationalists who were opposed to the new church objected on the grounds that local congregations could be bound by General Assembly decisions in which they had had no part, the number of such decisions in forty years could be counted on the fingers of one hand.

The union with the Congregational Union of Scotland in 2000 involved no changes in theology or polity. In this sense, it was less significant than the abolition of the District Councils six years later because that act removed a feature that had been a key element in the life of all of the constituent churches. Yet, even though the Scottish Churches of Christ had been part of the URC since 1981, the union in 2000 made the church aware of the issue of "one Church in three Nations," which was given new significance by the parliamentary devolution for Scotland and Wales in 1997. This situation has been further accentuated by recent divergences between the policies of the Westminster government and the authorities in Edinburgh and Cardiff.

Church and society

During the negotiating process, very little attention was paid to the changes that were taking place in the wider society (apart from the attempt to relate conciliar structures to the new local government boundaries that were established in 1974.) Yet, the period since the union has been dominated by such changes, rather than by internal theological issues. The fact of continuing numerical decline has dominated thinking. By 2013, the total number of members was roughly equivalent to those in the Presbyterian Church of England at the time of the union; even in the province where the numbers have declined the least, the percentage of the decline in forty years is 55 per cent and in some provinces the decline is over 80 per cent. There is no sense in which this is a consequence of the union; all of the churches in the UK have declined numerically, although some have decreased more than others. As indicated earlier, the decline in Congregationalism began before the First World War, and increased life expectancy has actually concealed the rate of decline by shifting the age balance of the church to people over sixty. The falling number of baptisms in the UK since the 1960s may have made the URC's baptismal policy more relevant to the changing mission situation.

The effects of this decline have been accentuated by changes in British towns, which have made life particularly difficult for congregations in the city centers, which had the largest numbers of members in the nineteenth century. Resources for building churches in new housing areas have been squeezed, and since 1945, new town planning legislation has made it more difficult to secure sites for church construction. Much effort has been put into ecumenical planning for new congregations. However, the ecumenical commitment of the URC may have worked to its disadvantage because a significant proportion of its congregations are now joint congregations with one or more other denominations. Although the URC has sought to fulfil its ecumenical vocation in this way, some have argued that this has been to its own detriment as a church. The question is: does this matter?

Social changes in family life and in attitudes toward divorce, remarriage, cohabitation, and sexuality have all crowded in on British churches during the period since the URC was formed. From its beginning, the URC has accepted divorced persons as members and ministers, and like other churches, it has had to come to terms with the fact that, for a variety of reasons, younger people often prefer to cohabit, rather than to marry, or chose to cohabit for several years before marrying. It has not always been easy to know how to adapt baptismal policy to these new patterns or to decide whether liturgical changes should be made in the recommended marriage service to reflect evolving understandings of marriage. Should the church recognize cohabiting couples by offering to bless their life together, and would such couples actually want such a blessing? When the question of homosexual relationships came to the fore in public discussion in the 1990s, the church set up a task force to consider the matter. After extensive consultations, it failed to produce agreement, and a seven-year moratorium on discussing this matter began. In 2007, the General Assembly made a commitment to recognize and respect the differences of opinion that existed within its ranks. For some people, these tensions were eased by the legislation that created civil partnerships; for others, however, even though that legislation removed anxieties about promiscuous relationships, it did not address the fundamental issue. In 2012, the Assembly's decision to permit such partnerships to be registered in a church if the local congregation wished to do so further complicated matters. The church's response to the same-sex marriage legislation of 2013 remains to be resolved. That will not be simple because in the case of marriage, the congregations appoint authorized persons to register the marriage; the case of civil partnerships, a civil registrar attends.

Church and state

These developments expose a further issue. In 1662, the predecessors of
the constituent parts of the URC left the Church of England rather than
accept legislative interference in the internal life of the church. However,
by the first decade of the twenty-first century, the church had gradually
accepted a degree of legislative interference in its affairs. This was partly
recognized at the time the church was formed. In 1972 (and again in 1981
and 2000), parliamentary legislation was required to make provisions for
the church property that had been held for the purposes of the constituent
churches to be used for the new church. However, unlike in the case of
Methodism for example, that legislation did not, in and of itself, create the
united church. That decision was made by the assemblies of the constituent
churches themselves. The act of Parliament addressed the necessary legal
implications of that decision.

Generally speaking, the range of the governmental legislation that has
affected the churches has increased since the 1990s. New employment
laws laid down detailed procedures for the dismissal of employees. Because ministers were regarded to be holders of an office, rather than employees, this law did not immediately affect the churches. However, it did
prompt greater consideration of procedures for ministerial discipline, and
that led the Assembly to act. Governmental concern about the viability of
pension programs led to legal adjudications by the pensions regulator that
required the church to increase its contributions. More recent legislation
about discrimination and equality has potential implications for a range of
issues that extend from ensuring disabled persons access to church buildings to being non-discriminatory with regard to issues related to sexuality.
Because of widespread protests, all churches were specifically exempted
from equality legislation in the case of decisions about same-sex marriage,
but some have wondered how far such exemptions can go and how long
they can last. What implications does such legislation have for the relations between even non-established churches and the state? Will a point
come when the right to religious liberty will clash with people's rights to
equal treatment before the law? In this whole discussion, broader changes
in the relative position of religion in British society are more relevant than
many people in the churches themselves realize or know how to handle.
Those changes mean that the nature of both division and unity in the church
is shifting. The question for our time is whether ecumenism can keep up
with these shifts.

Abbreviations

BU: Basis of Union.
URC: United Reformed Church.

Uniting for Unity, Reconciliation, and Justice: The Uniting Reformed Church in Southern Africa

Nico Koopman

1 Introduction

At its inception, the Protestant Church in The Netherlands (PCN) strove to actualize two central aims (among other objectives); namely, organic unity and being a suitable witness in the pluralistic arena of public life in the Netherlands. These two central aims coincide with the aims of the unification process of the Uniting Reformed Church in Southern Africa (URCSA). Thus, it is very interesting and important to compare the unification processes of the two churches ten years after the formation of the PCN and twenty years after the URCSA came into being.

The choice of the word "uniting" instead of "united" in the name of the URCSA has significance. Uniting refers to the awareness that the unification of the two churches that participated in the formation of the URCSA in April 1994 – namely, the former, mainly colored Dutch Reformed Mission Church (DRMC) and a major part of the former mainly black Dutch Reformed Church in Africa (DRCA) – has not been completed. Members of these two churches have had to continue actualizing the unity that was envisaged and advanced on the day the URCSA was formed. In the URCSA, we call this our internal unification process. Synods became one, presbyteries became one, and all of the ministries carried out at these levels became one. However, from our inception, we have had to ensure that the unity at the level of the broader church would also materialize in congregations whose boundaries remained unchanged after the merger. We have had to ensure that structural unity has indeed fostered existential unity.

Uniting also refers to our external unification process. Since our inception, we have been committed to external unification with other members
of what is called the Dutch Reformed Church family; namely, the Dutch
Reformed Church (DRC), which mainly has white members; the Reformed
Church in Africa (RCA), which mainly has Indian members, and the parts
of the DRCA that did not participate in the formation of the URCSA. We
are also committed to exploring unification with other Reformed churches
in Southern Africa, including one that broke away from the former DRMC
during apartheid, namely, the Calvin Protestant Church of South Africa.
Greater expressions of unity with other Reformed churches in other parts
of Africa, and especially in Southern Africa, is also envisaged, and we remain committed to building unity within the broader ecumenical family.

Unification refers to the URCSA's "public calling," as that was articulated in 1986 in the Confession of Belhar (BC) as adopted by the general
synod of the DRMC, at its meeting in Belhar. We expressly united in order
to work together for reconciliation in societies that had experienced – and
are still experiencing – enmity, alienation, and division. We are a uniting
church so that we can work for justice in contexts where we encounter the
biggest gaps in the world between the so-called haves and have-nots.

The next section of this essay will describe this public calling of the
URCSA. The three articles that make up the BC will constitute the theological framework for describing the URCSA's calling as a church. This discussion will then inform the final section of the paper, which will attempt
to assess the URCSA's progress in reaching its own aims. This assessment
will also pave the way for comparing the URCSA's progress with that of
the PCN. Some similarities and differences will be identified.

A short word about the Belhar Confession may be appropriate at this
point. In the former context of personal and structural violence; of racial
prejudice, apartheid, and apartheid theology; of separation and discrimination; of exclusion, alienation, and enmity; of injustice, humiliation, and
dehumanization; and of a threatened and challenged faith, a wonderful,
God-given event of consolation and comfort, of redemption and liberation,
of hope and healing appeared on our horizon. This gift was the declaration
of a *status confessionis* regarding these evils in 1982 and the adoption of
the BC in 1986.

In the *status confessionis*, the 1982 Synod of the former Dutch Reformed Mission Church courageously expressed the conviction – which
had also been expressed earlier in 1982 by the World Alliance of Reformed

Churches and in 1977 by the Lutheran World Federation – that the theological legitimation of apartheid's system of violence and violation of human dignity violated the heart of the gospel of Jesus Christ and posed a threat to the essence, nature, and credibility of the gospel. It was also stressed that where the Christian faith is threatened and challenged, it needs to be confessed afresh. Consequently, the DRMC decided to re-confess and reaffirm its faith in the triune God in this situation of grave threat to that faith.

The draft version of the BC was formulated by a committee whose central aim was simply to articulate and give expression to the faith that lived in the hearts of the DRMC's members. Jaap Durand, one of the members of the committee, suggested that the group should merely try to give voice to the faith that was incarnate within the DRMC. The drafting committee should be commended for taking this route, and we remain grateful to Dirkie Smit, the main author of the BC, for encapsulating, in an unforgettable way, the faith that resided within the hearts of the people of the DRMC. In 1982, at the very young age of thirty (!), he was already one of the best representatives of liberating Reformed theology in South Africa. The fact that his formulation was accepted by the DRMC with spontaneous affirmation and acclamation shows that the faith which sustained the people of the DRMC was not a parochial and provincial faith; at heart, it clearly was a Reformed faith. The continued positive reception of the BC by Reformed churches all over the world also bears witness to this observation, as does the fact that both old and young members of the DMRC recognized their deepest convictions in the words of the BC. It was those convictions that helped us resist apartheid with resilience and hope and eventually enabled us to overcome this evil system.

Against the backdrop of this brief sketch, it becomes clear why the BC constitutes such a crucial theological framework for understanding our public calling in post-apartheid South Africa.

2 Uniting for unity

Article 1 of the BC confesses faith in God, who is described as the One who unites his children. In the context of separation and discrimination on the basis of ethnicity (or any other criterion), we were (and may continue to be) strengthened by faith in the God who makes us one in the midst of all of our diversity. We are one family across all types of boundaries. As one family, we are equal in worth and dignity. As one family of God, we are equal in freedom. Over against separation and discrimination, we look up to a God who calls us to live in unity, which does not mean unity at a distance, but unity in proximity. The BC describes this unity as communion, as a means of sharing in each other's lives, and as living in solidarity and cohesion in a clear and challenging way. It states

that this unity of the people of God must be manifested and be active in a variety of ways: in that we love one another; that we experience, practice and pursue community with one another; that we are obligated to give ourselves willingly and joyfully to be of benefit and blessing to one another; that we share one faith, have one calling, are of one soul and one mind; have one God and Father, are filled with one Spirit, are baptized with one baptism, eat of one bread and drink of one cup, confess one Name, are obedient to one Lord, work for one cause, and share one hope; together come to know the height and the breadth and the depth of the love of Christ; together are built up to the stature of Christ, to the new humanity; together know and bear one another's burdens, thereby fulfilling the law of Christ that we need one another and upbuild one another, admonishing and comforting one another; that we suffer with one another for the sake of righteousness; pray together; together serve God in this world; and together fight against all which may threaten or hinder this unity (BC, § 2).

It is clear that the unity described in the BC is a unity in diversity, a unity despite past separation and enmity, a unity in freedom, and especially, a unity in constructive proximity. According to Dirkie Smit, the stress on the church's unity in the BC helps churches discover and confess that their continued disunity presents an obstacle to the quest for reconciliation and justice. This disunity implies the separation of people from different socio-economic groups who have different levels of privilege, training, skills, and participation and influence in society. Disunity represents the perpetuation of classism and a refusal to be involved with less privileged brothers and sisters. Smit writes in a remarkably compelling manner about the way in which the existence of separate churches and disunity prevents Christians from showing justice and compassion to one another. "Christians are denied the opportunity to get to know each other and to love and serve each other. Consequently it becomes more difficult – and usually almost impossible – to know and to carry each other's burdens" (see Smit 1984, 62). Therefore, the unity to which the URCSA is committed is a unity which implies that we are to search for reconciliation together and are to seek justice together.

3 Uniting for reconciliation

The reconciliation that is affirmed in the BC reflects the two dimensions of reconciliation that are found in Pauline thought. Reconciliation viewed as *hilasmos* has to do with the expiation of wrongs and stumbling blocks to atonement (at-one-ment). Reconciliation understood as *katalassoo* refers to harmony in one's relationship with the other. The type of reconciliation that the BC has in mind is the sort of embrace that Miroslav Volf advocates in his book *Exclusion and Embrace* (see Volf 1996, 171). He refers to the embrace of "normal" and disabled people and of persons belonging to different races, tribes, genders, nationalities, socio-economic groups, sexual orientations, and age groups. To this list, one could add human beings' embrace of nature. The reconciliation advocated by the BC pleads for the removal of stumbling blocks that stand in the way of peaceful living and embrace. Therefore, reconciliation involves opposition to various forms of alienation and enmity, which include racism, tribalism, xenophobia, classism, misogyny, homophobia, ageism, handicappism, ecocide, and similar patterns.

The significance of God's reconciliatory work in contexts of alienation and exclusion sustained us during the years of apartheid and enabled us to keep believing that reconciliation between people from diverse backgrounds – and between people who had lived in enmity – is possible. With Article 3 of the BC, we opposed any point of view that "is not prepared to venture on the road of obedience and reconciliation, but rather, out of prejudice, fear, selfishness and unbelief, denies in advance the reconciling power of the gospel."

Over against the exclusion of the other, the "Belhar faith" called for participation in each other's lives. One could even say that it called for participation in the affairs of public life, which is to say, in political, economic, and related spheres. Itumelang Mosala describes reconciliation as involving at-one-ment with the land, thus, he conveys this idea of participation in political and economic life which is signified by the notion of land (see Mosala 1987). Indeed, the BC spelled out the way for us to move from exclusion to embrace and participation.

4 Uniting for justice

The justice that is affirmed in the Belhar text is rightly described as compassionate justice. In line with the biblical use of these concepts, both the sacrificial and forensic dimensions of justice and justification are being referred to here. Through the redemptive work of Jesus Christ, God declares us to be just. People who have been justified by the grace of God participate in the quest for justice in the world. Justified people – that is, people who have been made right by the Triune God – seek human rights in our broken world.

According to Christopher Marshall, justification by faith is an expression of restorative justice (see Marshall 2001, 59). Thus, the notion of sacrificial justice has a second dimension, which shows that justice cannot be reached in this world when the willingness to make a sacrifice for the sake of the other is not present. A third aspect of the sacrificial dimension of justice involves the fact that justice does not seek revenge; rather, it is merciful. It seeks the healing and restoration of both perpetrators and victims. In fact, it seeks the healing of all broken relationships. Therefore, this justice is called restorative justice. In short, Marshal's analysis of the use of the word "justice" in the New Testament enables him to describe justice as being restorative or covenantal in nature. This covenantal justice goes beyond retribution and punishment, and, like reconciliation, seeks the healing of relationships. Like reconciliation, restorative and covenantal justice seeks to embrace. It seeks the renewal of the covenant between God and human beings, between human beings themselves, and between human beings and the rest of creation (see Marshall 2001, 35–93).

Amidst the injustices of apartheid in South Africa, the Holy Spirit enabled us to maintain our faith in the God who shows compassion to his people in special ways, especially in the case of those who are excluded, exploited, and marginalized. In South Africa, God's special identification with wronged people meant that he intervened and acted on their behalf. Exodus 3 verses 7 to 22 expresses both these dimensions of compassion and action for justice clearly. He sought the redemption and restoration of the victims, perpetrators, and beneficiaries of unjust practices.

5 Stocktaking?

The last part of this paper will assess the URCSA's progress with regard to its twofold aim of unification and public witness. How has the URCSA fared with regard to both the internal and external unification processes? How has the URCSA fared with regard to its public witness in the context of a young democracy? How do the URCSA's quests relate to those of the PCN?

5.1 Internal unification?

At the level of meetings of the broader church – namely, the general synod, regional synod and presbytery – the structures of the two uniting churches have become one. The various ministries on these levels have also become one. This structural unity is quite positive and contributes to our sense of organic unity and solidarity with each other. Meetings and worship opportunities on these levels typically are diverse in style and language. However, the experience is always one of joy at togetherness in diversity. The diversity of the ethnic and socio-economic groups involved in such gatherings reflects the diverse nature of the society of which we are part. The various needs and challenges that characterize this diverse society are also present in the URCSA and are being dealt with by this church of diversity. The unity in diversity which is present in the URCSA reflects the unity in diversity of the eschatological community to which the Spirit is leading the church.

It would not be wrong to conclude that we have made tremendous progress building internal unity at the level of the broader church. However, our internal unity at the level of local congregations still reflects the highly color-based composition of South African neighborhoods. The Group Areas Act, which divided neighborhoods along ethnic lines, was one of the pillars of apartheid in South Africa. Although integration is occurring gradually, its impact has not yet been strong enough to diversify local congregations. Due to language challenges, the calling of black pastors to congregations that mainly have colored members, and vice versa, does not take place.

One may argue that it is important to ensure that people are still able to worship in their mother tongue and in their preferred worship style on the local level, but it is also important to ensure that there is more interaction among the congregants. More joint worship services need to be held

by the congregations on a regular basis, and a higher degree of consideration needs to be given to greater collaboration among congregations than
currently is the case.

5.2 External unification?

The external unification process has mainly been focused on unification
with the other members of the DRC family. This has been an ambivalent
journey characterized by progress in some respects and setbacks in other
regards. Various ministries of the URCSA and the DRC are already united
in a collaborative way, and various unifying initiatives are taking place on
synodal, presbyterial, and congregational levels. The DRC's positive conclusions about the BC have enhanced unification processes within the DRC
family.

5.3 Public witness?

To a great extent, the URCSA has fulfilled its public witness with regard to
its priestly task to care for people and to address various forms of broken-
ness and alienation. The URCSA has also fulfilled its kingly servant task to
nurture hope and to foster a culture of ethical and responsible discipleship,
citizenship, and leadership in our young democracy.

Like all other churches in South Africa, the URCSA is struggling to
give voice to its prophetic stance in this new context where it is not sufficient to spell out broad visions of a new society and to offer criticism when
this vision is betrayed. We also need to participate in policy-making and
policy-implementation processes that require thorough methodical analy-
ses of political, economic, and related issues. More needs to be done with
regard to our prophetic task in the public arena.

5.4 The URCSA and the PCN

There are striking similarities between the quests for unification that the
URCSA and the PCN have undertaken. For example:
- Both churches have set the goal of building an organic, concrete, visible,
  and lived unity.
- Both churches have committed themselves to fulfilling their public vo-
  cation in rapidly changing societies.
- Both churches acknowledge that without this lived unity, our witness in
  the public sphere is inhibited and without credibility.

– Both churches have articulated the desire to build a unity that will guard against individualism and collectivism. We want a unity that makes room for communion, togetherness, and social cohesion. However, this communion should also make room for the needs of the individual, for the individual's life *coram Deo*.
– Both churches focus on the notion of going back to the roots, as this is spelled out in the November 2011 vision paper of the PCN, which is entitled *The Heartbeat of Life* (see above, 41). This notion entails adherence and faithfulness to the rich Christian tradition. However, this focus on tradition does not foster a traditionalism that is not open to the renewal and transformation of church and society. A focus on tradition is mandated by the conviction that the Christian tradition does have insights which are indispensable for contemporary personal, church, and public life.
– Both churches must build an ethos of tolerance and embrace amidst the plurality of doctrinal and ethical positions that exist among their members, concerning, for example, the ordination and marriage of our gay and lesbian brothers and sisters.
– Both churches are called to witness faithfully in rapidly changing public contexts and in societies that are facing immense challenges.
– Both churches are addressing questions regarding identity: the identity of the individual, the identity of the church (especially of the local church), and the identity of a broader society which remains in a state of change and transition and is difficult to comprehend. In addition, both churches are posing questions about of the role of confessions of faith in this discourse about identity. In the case of the URCSA, the 1986 Confession of Belhar fulfills an informative, illuminating, inspiring, and transformative role in its discussions about the identity of the URCSA and the identity of the broader South African society.

The contexts of and specific challenges facing these two churches differ, but it is very interesting to note the similarities. Arjan Plaisier's plea (see above, 48) is as relevant for the URCSA as it is for the PCN, namely, that in the face of all of our challenges, we make room for mourning; for *metanoia*; for confessing sin, laziness, and self-sufficiency; and for new openness to our Lord Jesus Christ, to hope, and to new opportunities!

Abbreviations and bibliography

BC: Belhar Confession.
DRC: Dutch Reformed Church.
DRCA: Dutch Reformed Church in Africa.
DRMC: Dutch Reformed Mission Church.
PCN: Protestant Church in the Netherlands.
RCA: Reformed Church in Africa.
URCSA: Uniting Reformed Church in Southern Africa.

Marshall, Christopher. 2001. Beyond Retribution: A New Testament Vision for Justice, Crime and Punishment. Grand Rapids: Eerdmans.
Mosala, Itumelang. 1987. The Meaning of Reconciliation: A Black Perspective. In: Journal of Theology for Southern Africa, 59(1987), 19–25.
Smit, Dirk J. 1984. "... op 'n besondere wyse die God van die noodlydende, die arme en die veronregte ...". In: G. Daan Cloete, and Dirk J. Smit (eds.), A moment of truth, Grand Rapids MI: Eerdmans , 62–75, 143–159.
Volf, Miroslav. 1996. Exclusion and Embrace. A Theological Exploration of Identity, Otherness and Reconciliation. Nashville: Abingdon Press.

We are a Pilgrim People:
The Uniting Church in Australia

Andrew Dutney

The Uniting Church in Australia (UCA) was inaugurated on June 22, 1977. The negotiations that led to this union were initiated twenty years earlier in 1957 with the formation of the Joint Commission on Church Union by the Congregational, Methodist, and Presbyterian churches. This commission was established to lead a consultative process that would identify a basis on which the three denominations could unite. It issued two reports – *The Faith of the Church* (1959) and *The Church: Its Nature, Function and Ordering* (1963) – and two proposals (1963 and 1970) on the way to publishing the Basis of Union (1971) that eventually would be voted on by the three denominations and become the foundation document of the UCA.

It was quite a journey, but it came at the end of an even longer journey towards church union in Australia – which began in the last half of the nineteenth century! Indeed, Presbyterianism came to Australia in three divided denominations: the Church of Scotland, the Free Church of Scotland, and the United Presbyterian Church. In Victoria, the Free Church managed to split into two synods, and the United Presbyterian split into three synods. Thus by the 1850s, there were six Presbyterian denominations in Victoria and a similarly splintered church in the other Australian colonies. The first reunion of Presbyterian churches anywhere in the world took place in Victoria in 1859. Presbyterians in the other colonies pursued the same goal, with the final reunion taking place in Western Australia in 1901. However, these Presbyterian churches were still divided by the borders of the colonies. In 1884, the separate churches joined in a federal union which approved a scheme for organic union in 1894, but that had to wait until 1901 for the Presbyterian Church of Australia to become a reality.

Originally, there were five separate Methodist denominations in Australia too: the Wesleyan Methodist Church, the Primitive Methodist Church, the United Methodist Free Church, the Bible Christian Church, and a very small contingent of the Methodist New Connexion. Between 1888 and 1901, these separated Methodist churches were gradually reunited, and in May 1904, the First General Conference of the Methodist Church of Australia was held in Melbourne.

In 1901, the first Assembly of the Presbyterian Church of Australia affirmed its "sympathy with the great ideal of a United Evangelical Church of Australia" and appointed a committee "to consider the principles on which the Presbyterian Church of Australia [would be] prepared to consider the question of a larger union." An overture was made to other denominations, and by the next Assembly in 1903, conversations had been taking place with the Anglican, Baptist, Congregational, and Methodist churches.

From that time until the Joint Commission on Church Union was formed in 1957, there were seven series of church union negotiations involving different combinations of the denominations which would eventually form the UCA. These negotiations produced five different schemes of union. Two united churches were formed – the United Church of North Australia (1956) and the United Church in Papua New Guinea and the Solomon Islands (1962).

It had been quite a journey indeed by the time of the inauguration of the UCA in 1977. It is hardly surprising, then, that there is a "journey" theme in the UCA's Basis of Union (BU). Yet, it is not, as might be expected, a theme celebrating this church union as the journey's end, the task completed, the story concluded. On the contrary, the Basis of Union emphasizes that being on a journey is the normal condition of the church of God.

The church is a pilgrim people

Throughout the UCA's Basis of Union, the church's existence is imagined as a journey, a movement, a process of ongoing exploration and change – on the way to a known goal – which is described as "that coming reconciliation and renewal which is the end in view for the whole creation" (BU, § 3). This is evident in paragraph 1. There, the churches that entered the union affirmed their sense of being a people on a journey, not yet at their destination. These churches "look for a continuing renewal"; "declare their readiness to go forward together"; "remain open to constant reform"; and "seek a wider unity." In the last sentences of the Basis of Union, the theme is still there:

The Uniting Church affirms that it belongs to the people of God on the way to the promised end. The Uniting Church prays that, through the gift of the Holy Spirit, God will constantly correct that which is erroneous in its life, will bring it into deeper unity with other Churches, and will use its worship, witness and service to God's eternal glory through Jesus Christ the Lord. Amen (BU, § 18).

However, the key crystallization of this theme is in paragraph 3:

The Church lives between the time of Christ's death and resurrection and the final consummation of all things which Christ will bring; the Church is a pilgrim people, always on the way towards a promised goal; here the Church does not have a continuing city but seeks one to come. On the way Christ feeds the Church with Word and Sacraments, and it has the gift of the Spirit in order that it may not lose the way (BU, § 3).

Davis McCaughey, one of the key contributors to the drafting of the document, was very clear about the centrality of this theme: "There is nothing more important said about the Church anywhere in the Basis of Union than in these sentences" (McCaughey 1980, 21). This being so, there is no better place to begin to understand the UCA's vision and vocation than with this metaphor: "The Church is a pilgrim people."

The church is not what it ought to be

Although it is familiar language these days, the description of the church as "a pilgrim people" is quite strange. It first appeared in the early 1950s in very specific circumstances. There is, of course, an ancient tradition of Christian pilgrimage. However, the sixteenth century Protestant movement condemned pilgrimages as superstition and "works righteousness," and did their best to eradicate them. The word was preserved in later Protestant piety (e.g. the "pilgrim fathers" or John Bunyan's *Pilgrim's Progress*), but only in a very individualized sense. It wasn't used of the church as a whole.

The nearest idiom was "the church militant" (as contrasted to "the church triumphant"), although the images of the church as an army and the church as a group of pilgrims clash. There was a biblical precedent – if only in the King James Version, where the forebears of faith are called "pilgrims on the earth" (Hebrews 11:13), and Canaan is promised as "the land of their pilgrimage" (Exodus 6:4). But that's it. The image of the church as a pilgrim was essentially unprecedented when it appeared in the early 1950s.

The phrase was popularized by Marcus Ward in 1953, in the title of his book *The Pilgrim Church: An Account of the First Five Years of the Church of South India*, which was read throughout the world and became a classic work in the fields of mission and ecumenism. The Church of South India (CSI) was formed in 1947 in a controversial union that brought Anglican, Congregational, Methodist, and Presbyterian churches together in a scheme that made some vital elements an *outcome* of, rather than a *precondition* for, union.

It is striking that Ward never actually used the term "pilgrim" anywhere in the text of his book, *The Pilgrim Church*. It is only in the title. It was not part of the theological vocabulary of that time. It still had a whiff of "popery" about it, so Ward was not confident about using it. Even in the introduction, he accounted for the odd title of his book without ever using the word "pilgrim!" There, he explained that in 1950, when the Theological Commission of the CSI considered an invitation to contribute to an international symposium on the "Nature of the Church,"

the Church of South India represented a venture of Christian reunion of a kind that had not previously been attempted. ... It seemed too soon for the new Church to attempt to contribute anything permanent or significant to ecumenical discussions. One member used the phrase "a Church on the wing" to express our sense of being a Church *in via*, in movement but not yet having arrived. The idea was written into the chapter produced by the Commission ... (Ward 1953, 10f.).

From the time of that international meeting and the requested report on the experiences that the CSI had undergone during the first few years of its life, the idea of the church as a whole being on a pilgrimage began to capture the imagination of the ecumenical mission movement.

If Marcus Ward was shy about using the term he accidentally popularized, his CSI colleague, Lesslie Newbigin had no qualms at all. Newbigin was a new CSI bishop, a prominent younger leader in the World Council of Churches that had been formed in 1948, and a persuasive proponent of the integration of the World Council of Churches and the International Missionary Council (which would take place in 1961). He articulated the ecumenical vision of the church in the mission of God when it was new, sharp, energizing, and irresistible to that generation – which was the very generation that included those who would, in due course, form the Uniting Church in Australia. In 1952, Newbigin delivered a series of lectures that were published the following year as a collection entitled *The Household of God*.

Newbigin said that "perhaps the most important thing" about the Constitution of the CSI "is the explicit confession that *the Church is not what it ought to be*." He wrote:

The Church is the pilgrim people of God. It is on the move – hastening to the ends of the earth to beseech all men [sic] to be reconciled to God, and hastening to the end of time to meet its Lord who will gather all into one. Therefore the nature of the Church is never to be finally defined in static terms, but only in terms of that to which it is going. It cannot be understood rightly except in a perspective which is at once missionary and eschatological. ... *When the church ceases to be one, or ceases to be missionary, it contradicts its own nature.* Yet the Church is not defined by what it is, but by that End to which it moves, the power of which now works in the Church, the power of the Holy Spirit which is the earnest of the inheritance still to be revealed (Newbigin 1953, 25f.).

By 1954, at the Second Assembly of the WCC in Evanston, the official report included a long section under the heading "The Pilgrim People of God." The theme was also important at the Third Assembly in New Delhi in 1961 and again at the Fourth Assembly in Uppsala in 1968. It also found its way into the revolutionary statements of Vatican II, where it is discussed in Article 8 of *Lumen gentium* and in Article 4 of the Decree on Ecumenism.

The final drafts of the Basis of Union were completed in 1968 at the very time that the image of the church as a pilgrim people had secured its place in the vocabulary of faith.

There are several important features of the way this image is used in the Basis of Union and in the UCA.

– It is God's Church as a whole which is described as "a pilgrim people," called through Abraham, empowered at Pentecost, and living in anticipation of "the final consummation of all things that Christ will bring" (BU, § 3).

– The UCA "belongs" to that pilgrim people along with every other Christian fellowship, – be it Catholic, Indigenous, Protestant, Orthodox, or Pentecostal.

- The end or goal of that pilgrimage is "that reconciliation and renewal which is the end in view for the whole creation" (BU, § 3). As a fellowship of the Holy Spirit, the Church is a foretaste, sign, and instrument of that end.
- In view of that end, denominational forms, customs, and habits are transient. They are gifts intended to sustain the pilgrimage during its different stages. A continual process of discernment is required of each Christian fellowship in order for it to recognize the gifts of the Spirit that have been provided for this day and to obtain release from the futile effort to recover gifts that were meant for a past day.

"When the church ceases to be one or missionary it contradicts its own nature"

In the lectures that he gave in 1952, Newbigin defined the Church as:

a visible company in every place of all who confess Jesus as Lord, abiding together in the Apostles' teaching and fellowship, the breaking of bread, and the prayers. ... Its form is the visible fellowship, not of those whom we choose out to be our friends, but of those whom God has actually given to us as our neighbours. It is therefore simply humanity in every place re-created in Christ. (Newbigin 1953, 21)

This understanding of the church was echoed a decade later in the second report of the Joint Commission on Church Union:

The Church in one region, in fellowship with other regional churches, has been regarded from the beginning as embodying the fullness of the Church's life (1 Cor. 1:2). A congregation gathered by God in one place and living by his Word and sacraments in godly discipline, was and ever has been the characteristic expression of the life of the Church. ... Here is the relationship of believers in which men, women and children alike are called to recognize each other as loved creatures, and to allow God in Christ to break down every barrier that divides, so that they may participate in, and show to the world, the unity of their life in the family of God (JCCU 1963, 123).

Yet, there also appears to be a subtle narrowing of vision in the Joint Commission's version of this ecumenical consensus. Whereas Newbigin spoke of "a visible company in every place of all who confess Jesus as Lord," the Joint Commission refers instead to "a congregation."

Literally speaking, "a visible company in [one] place of all who confess Jesus as Lord" would be "a congregation," but in the towns and suburbs of Australia in the 1960s, a congregation shared its locale with a multitude of other Christian congregations from which it was divided. In practice, the "relationship of believers" did not extend to believers in the other congregations in that place. Nonetheless within each of those separate congregations, "men, women and children alike [were] called to recognize each other as loved creatures, and to allow God in Christ to break down every barrier that divides." Furthermore, the purpose of church union was to call the members of Congregational, Methodist, and Presbyterian congregations "in every place" to respond to that call in relation to one another. There was a hope and expectation among those who led the church union movement that, through the work of the Holy Spirit, ways would eventually be found to cross the rest of the denominational boundaries "in every place" and to make the unity of the church truly "visible."

By the time the Uniting Church was finally formed in 1977, no one still believed that formal church union would be one of the ways (let alone the primary way) that this vision of "a visible company in every place of those who confess Jesus as Lord" would be realized. Although there was no consensus on what other ways of expressing Christian unity beyond our own organization were coming to hand, there were several of these to pursue, such as:

– continued commitment to local, regional, national, and international ecumenical organizations;
– partnerships with churches of similar traditions in other countries, especially in Asia and the Pacific;
– coalitions with agencies of other denominations around particular concerns, such as peacemaking, gambling, or the fair treatment of asylum seekers;
– negotiations with partner churches overseas, such as Presbyterian and Methodist denominations in Korea, Tonga, or Fiji, regarding the need for the Uniting Church to provide support and oversight for their congregations in Australia;
– extending the hospitality and support of the UCA to groups of Christians of diverse cultural and linguistic backgrounds that are part of a dozen "national conferences," many of which include members of denominations that are divided in their country of origin;

- encouragement of non-denominational resourcing and renewal movements, such as Willow Creek's Global Leadership Summit, Taizé worship, Mission-Shaped Ministry, and Messy Church;
- participation and leadership in many different local interdenominational initiatives in witness and service.

The church in the essential biblical form that was envisioned by the ecumenical mission movement of the 1950s and 1960s was utterly at odds with denominationalism – and it still is!

Rather than "a visible company in every place of all who confess Jesus as Lord," we are used to single postcodes crammed with different denominations distinguished from each other by heritage, style, language, ethnicity, socio-economic status, and so forth. Far from being "the visible fellowship ... of those whom God has actually given us," we form like-minded, like-mannered gatherings that suit us even better than the lottery of our immediate families. Instead of seeking humanity in every place [being] re-created in Christ" we perpetuate all of the divisions of the surrounding society, and even add a few of our own from previous centuries.

In 1947, the CSI was formed as a refusal to perpetuate the sad sham of denominationalism in India, where Christianity was a minority faith bearing witness in one of the largest nations on earth. In 1977, the UCA was formed in an act of commitment to the goal of God's mission, which is "that coming reconciliation and renewal which is the end in view for the whole creation." Neither union expected to be the last word on the true form of the church. Both saw union as an instance of re-embarking on the journey as part of the pilgrim people of God.

"The Uniting Church affirms that it belongs to the people of God on the way to the promised end" (BU, § 18). We *belong* to that pilgrim people; we don't *constitute* it. Belonging to that people relativizes our particular organization's claims to "that coming reconciliation and renewal which is the end in view for the whole creation." This means that our commitment to being "a fellowship of reconciliation" is not primarily based on a desire for the UCA to become more diverse and inclusive, but for the church be more visibly *one*. By the power of the gospel, the church of God is already gloriously multicultural, multigenerational, multilingual, and multiethnic – especially in Australia – but we are divided. Our divisions conceal the sign and foretaste of "that coming reconciliation and renewal" which God has already given through the church. The challenge is not so much for the UCA to be multicultural and so forth, but for it to be more visibly *one*. Then it will become clear that the life we have in Christ already "transcends cultural and economic, national and racial boundaries" (BU, § 2).

Church unions still happen sometimes, but we can't put all our eggs in that basket. There are many other ways "to bear witness to that unity which is both Christ's gift and his will for the Church" (BU, § 1). For now, among the pilgrim people of God, it is a virtue to be careless about our denominational boundaries and a sign of maturity to be reckless in extending hospitality and cooperation to other denominations in a demonstration of "humanity in every place re-created in Christ."

Abbreviations and bibliography

BU:	Basis of Union.
CSI:	Church of South India.
JCCU 1963:	The Church: Its Nature, Function and Ordering, the Second Report of the Joint Commission on Church Union. In: Bos and Thompson (eds.). 2008, 69–186.
UCA:	Uniting Church in Australia.
WCC:	World Council of Churches.

Bos, Robert, and Geoff Thompson (eds.). 2008. Theology for Pilgrims: Selected Theological Documents of the Uniting Church in Australia. Sydney: Uniting Church Press.

McCaughey, J. Davis. 1980, Commentary on the Basis of Union, Melbourne: Uniting Church Press.

Newbigin, Lesslie. 1953. The Household of God: Lectures on the Nature of the Church. London: SCM Press Ltd.

Ward, Marcus. 1953. The Pilgrim Church: An Account of the First Five Years in the Life of the Church of South India. London: The Epworth Press.

Part III

Reflections

The Identity of the Church and Christian Unity

William Henn

One of the most encouraging aspects of the contributions to the present book – *The Protestant Church in the Netherlands: Church Unity in the 21st Century* – is their unabashed conviction that visible unity is not only desirable, but is also necessary, if currently divided Christian communities wish to be faithful to Christ's will for the Church. Moreover, these essays show that, at least to a certain extent, such unity is possible! The Protestant Church in the Netherlands, along with the united or uniting churches in Belgium, the United Kingdom, Southern Africa, and Australia, have all undertaken the courageous and arduous process of journeying together to a fully united community, which some of the contributions even speak of in terms of "visible" or "organic" unity. In the following essay, I would like to recall, first, their motivation for seeking unity; second, some ways in which Christian and ecclesial identity relates to church unity and; third, how a recent multi-lateral convergence statement outlining a "common vision of the Church" might – in the years ahead – serve to assist further efforts to promote unity among churches that are still divided.

Why a united church?

The motivation for this journey to unity has been expressed eloquently in the Declaration of Intent that is cited in Leo Koffeman's chapter on the birth of the PCN:

We would increase our guilt towards God and our fellow human beings if we were content with this division. ... We no longer want to set over against each other the different forms of being church which have taken shape in time, in which we went separate ways, but in obedience to the Lord of the Church we want to introduce them into a process of reunion and renewal (see above, 14).

The Declaration on Unification of December 12, 2003, added:

We unite believing that *our Lord Jesus Christ* himself prayed for the unity of his Church, so that the world may believe in Him. The separate roads which our churches in the Netherlands have been following since the Reformation in the 16th century and the two secessions in the 19th century, meet here (see above, 31).

Other united or uniting churches offer similar statements. Hugh Robert Boudin closes his account of the origin of the United Protestant Church in Belgium by asking "why this unification happened." Not, he replies, 'simply to conform to the spirit of the times, to do what everyone else was doing, to become more powerful, or to form a united front, but rather for the sole purpose of rendering better witness to the gospel of our Lord' (see above, 75). Regarding the United Reformed Church of the United Kingdom, David Thompson quotes a key paragraph from the *Statement on the Nature, Faith, and Order of the United Reformed Church*, which declares that "the Lord Jesus Christ, the only ruler and head of the Church, has therein appointed a government distinct from civil government and in things spiritual not subordinate thereto" (see above, 82). This statement points to the notion that Christ's design for the Church serves as a fundamental motivation for seeking unity, as Nico Koopman's contribution also does. Koopman notes that Article 1 of the Belhar Confession (BC) of 1986 confesses faith in God as the One who unites his children. He adds: "The BC describes this unity as communion, as a means of sharing in each other's lives, and as living in solidarity and cohesion in a clear and challenging way" (see above, 94). A pertinent passage from the Confession itself states

that this unity of the people of God must be manifested and be active in a variety of ways: in that we love one another; that we experience, practice and pursue community with one another; that we are obligated to give ourselves willingly and joyfully to be of benefit and blessing to one another; that we share one faith, have one calling, are of one soul and one mind; have one God and Father, are filled with one Spirit, are baptized with one baptism, eat of one bread and drink of one cup, confess one Name, are obedient to one Lord, work for one cause, and share one hope; together come to know the height and the breadth and the depth of the love of Christ; together are built up to the stature of Christ, to the new humanity; together know and bear one another's burdens, thereby fulfilling the law of Christ that we need one another and upbuild one another, admonishing and comforting one another; that we suffer with one another for the sake of righteousness; pray together; together serve God in this world; and together fight against all which may threaten or hinder this unity (BC, art. 2).

This beautiful and exquisite crescendo of characteristics not only echoes many passages of the New Testament which speak of the unity of the Church; it also reminds one of some of the classic statements about "the unity we seek" that were approved at several meetings of the General Assembly of the World Council of Churches, such as those which were held in New Delhi (1963), Nairobi (1975), Canberra (1990), and Porto Alegre (2006).

One of the evident gains produced by the ecumenical movement, – which began a little over a hundred years ago – is the creation of an atmosphere of fellowship and friendship among large segments of the populations of many, although not all, Christian communities. However, one unintended negative consequence of this gain may be the fact that many now feel less need for the actual unification of churches that are currently divided from one another. Amicable collaboration without resolving division seems to be "enough" for some. This development finds expression in some of the questions that Koffeman poses in his concluding evaluative remarks: "Why are we so focused on organic unity? What exactly is decisive for our unity: only church order or also real communion in confessing our faith together?"

The answer to such questions evokes reflections on the very *identity* of the Church. I found Arjan Plaisier's essay on "The Heartbeat of the Life of the Protestant Church" to be very stimulating in opening the door to answering some of these questions. In a section entitled "Back to the Roots," Plaisier writes:

Going back to the origins also means getting a renewed vision – a new image – of the church. In this case, this image will not be a sheer invention, only a product of our intuition or creative imagination. First and foremost, it will involve rediscovering what we are as a church, what makes the church, or better yet, *who* makes the church. ... This will be possible only by our "being made church" again, and that is not in our hands; it is in the Lord's hand. Nevertheless, this will not happen unless we once again realize what the church is, to whom the church belongs, and how we may live that reality. That is the reason for the movement back to the roots (see above, 41f.).

The four "We's" (Aristotelian, Cartesian, Stoic, and Epicurean) described by Harm Dane (see above, 52ff.), as well as the "pilgrim people" discussed by Andrew Dutney (see above, 102ff.), also seem to take up themes deeply related to the question of the identity of the Christian community For this reason, the remainder of my essay is intended to be a brief reflection on Christian and ecclesial identity, especially as they relate to the unity of the Church.

Identity and unity

One way of going "back to the roots" in order to uncover our identity as Christians and as church would be to consider again some of the insights of our forebears in the faith. Given both the limited number of words allotted for my contribution and the presumed ecclesial affiliation of a large portion of its readership, perhaps it would be reasonable to begin with a few insights from John Calvin.

Surely a privileged source for his insights into the nature and mission of the Church is Book IV of his *Institutes of the Christian Religion*, which bears the title "The External Means or Aids by Which God Invites Us into the Society of Christ and Holds Us Therein." Calvin begins his discussion of the Church with the fundamental principle that it is by faith in the gospel and not by works of the law that one comes to be in communion with Christ and to be saved. Because of their weakness, human beings need help to come to such faith and God, in his sovereign providence, offers such help. To insure that they hear effective preaching of the good news, God has deposited the precious treasure of the Gospel within the Church, appointing pastors and teachers to proclaim it with authority. In addition, God has instituted the sacraments, which are "most useful helps in fostering and confirming our faith" (Calvin 1559, IV, 1.1). God's children are entrusted to the maternal care of the Church so that they may grow to the perfection of faith. The role of the Church as teacher is underscored:

Paul says that our Savior "ascended far above all heavens, that he might fill all things. And he gave some, apostles; and some, prophets; and some evangelists; and some, pastors and teachers; for the perfecting of the saints, for the work of the ministry, for the edifying of the body of Christ: till we all come in the unity of the faith, and of the knowledge of the Son of God, unto a perfect man, unto the measure of the stature of the fullness of Christ" (Eph. 4:10–13). We see that God, who might perfect his people in a moment, chooses not to bring them to manhood in any other way than by the education of the Church. We see the mode of doing it expressed; the preaching of celestial doctrine is committed to pastors. We see that all without exception are brought into the same order, that they may with meek and docile spirit allow themselves to be governed by teachers appointed for this purpose (Calvin 1559, IV, 1.5).

Calvin applies Jesus' saying about the indissolubility of marriage to the Church: "'What God has thus joined let not man put asunder' (Mark 10:9); to those to whom he is a Father, the Church must also be a mother," a phrase which echoes a passage from St. Cyprian of Carthage (Calvin 1559, IV, 1.1). The theme of the Church as mother who brings up children in the faith seems to me to be a very important aspect of Calvin's ecclesiology and one of his reasons for affirming the traditional principle concerning the necessity of the Church for salvation: "the abandonment of the Church is always fatal" (Calvin 1559, IV, 1.4).

I believe that in this summary of some ecclesial notions from the beginning of Book IV of the *Institutes*, one can discern a parallel to the description of the Church in Article 4 of the Lutheran *Augsburg Confession*. The article identifies the Church as being present whenever the Gospel is preached in its purity and the sacraments are celebrated according to the New Testament. In Calvin's thought, both the Word of God and the sacraments are essential elements of the Church. However, as the aforementioned quotation shows, he was also very insistent on the important role that ordained ministers serve in teaching and guiding the community. This leads me to believe that one way of expressing the essential components of ecclesial unity can be derived from the description that portrays Christ and of his followers in terms of the three functions that the Old Testament understood to be part of God's providential way of maintaining the people of Israel. These roles are each associated with an anointing and are typically represented by the designation prophet, priest and king. The fact that the Church is a community of the Word reflects Christ's function as prophet (see Luke 4:17–19). The fact that it celebrates baptism and the Lord's Supper and calls upon disciples to offer their lives as a spiritual sacrifice reflects Christ's priestly role (see Rom. 12:1, Hebrews 5:1–10). The service of believers – either by way of various ordained and non-ordained ministries within the church or through service beyond the church in the areas of evangelization and promoting justice and peace – reflects Jesus' role as the servant king who inaugurates the kingdom of God (see Mark 1:14–15). Nico Koopman refers explicitly to these three functions in his essay on the Uniting Reformed Church in Southern Africa (see above, 98.).

In this regard, the Heidelberg Catechism contains the following questions and answers concerning the identity of Christ and of his followers, which may serve as a kind of confirmation of the proposal that one of the ways of understanding the identity of the Christian community may be found in thinking of the Church as being the prophetic, priestly, and royal (servant) people of God.

Q&A 31 – Q: Why is he called "Christ," meaning "anointed?" A: Because he has been ordained by God the Father and has been anointed with the Holy Spirit (Luke 3:21–22; 4:14–19 [Isa. 61:1], Heb. 1:9 [Ps. 45:7]) to be our chief prophet and teacher (Acts 3:22 [Deut. 18:15]) who fully reveals to us the secret counsel and will of God concerning our deliverance (John 1:18; 15:15); our only high priest (Heb. 7:17 [Ps. 110:4]) who has delivered us by the one sacrifice of his body (Heb. 9:12; 10:11–14), and who continually pleads our cause with the Father (Rom. 8:34; Heb. 9:24), and our eternal King (Matt. 21:5 [Zech. 9:9]) who governs us by his Word and Spirit, and who guards us and keeps us in the freedom he has won for us (Matt. 28:18–20; John 10:28; Rev. 12:10–11).

Q&A 32 – Q: But why are you called a Christian? A: Because by faith I am a member of Christ (1 Cor. 12:12–27) and so I share in his anointing (Acts 2:17 [Joel 2:28]; 1 John 2:27). I am anointed to confess his name (Matt. 10:32; Rom. 10:9–10; Heb. 13:15), to present myself to him as a living sacrifice of thanks (Rom. 12:1; 1 Pet. 2:5:9), to strive with a free conscience against sin and the devil in this life (Gal. 5:16–17; Eph. 6:11; 1 Tim. 1:18–19), and afterward to reign with Christ over all creation for eternity (Matt. 25:34; 2 Tim. 2:12).

What might one say about the identity of the Church in the light of such passages? Like its Lord and Savior, the Church is prophetic, priestly, and royal (in the sense that to serve is to reign). This triad expresses what might be called the very core of the identity of the Christian community. In following the Christ who is prophet, priest, and royal servant, the church must be a community of witness (*martyria*) to the truth of the gospel; a community of worship (*leiturgia*) as it celebrates baptism, the Lord's Supper, and other rites; and a community of service (*diakonia*), both within the church through the various ministries that are needed for its peaceful functioning and externally, through the work of proclaiming the message of the gospel in words (evangelization) and in deeds (acting on behalf of justice, peace, and the protection of the environment). This triad of activities – proclaiming the Word in witness; celebrating the sacraments in worship; and working for the cause of justice, peace, and the protection of creation in service – corresponds to the identity of the Church as a prophetic, priestly, and royal servant community patterned after the example of Christ, the prophet, priest and king whose body the Church was created to be. Christian communities which are currently divided not only may *choose* to become united in visible, organic unity; I believe that, in obedience to the will of Christ, they have a *duty* to do so whenever they arrive at a certain "critical mass" of common understanding and self-conscious expression of their identity as a prophetic (faithful), priestly (sacramental) and royal servant (ministering) people.

"The Church: Towards a Common Vision"

Of course, this triad does not exhaust the ways in which the identity of the Church can be expressed. Thus, in recent years, theologians have devoted much attention to describing the Christian community in terms of the inseparable notions of communion and mission. These two themes are combined very nicely in the marvelous opening verses of the First Letter of John, which include these words. "That which we have seen and heard we proclaim to you [mission] so that you may have fellowship with us [communion] and our fellowship is with the Father and with his Son Jesus Christ." Yet, it seems to me that both mission and communion are made possible and brought into existence precisely through the operation of the Holy Spirit, which fashions the community as a prophetic, priestly, and royal body. Word, sacrament, and service give birth to the Church day by day. They create communion and provide the essential components of mission.

Recently, the Faith and Order Commission of the World Council of Churches published a new statement entitled *The Church: Towards a Common Vision*. At the time of its publication, it was maintained that, as a "convergence" text, this document could provide valuable aid to Christians who want to draw closer in their understanding of the "society of Christ into which God invites and [holds] them," to use the expression from the beginning of Book IV of Calvin's *Institutes*. The convergence statement has four chapters, the first and last of which place special emphasis on the Church's mission of proclaiming the gospel and seeking to serve as an instrument in Christ's hands for healing a world broken by sin and injustice. The middle two chapters focus more on communion. In particular, the second chapter highlights how much Christians already share

in their vision of the Church by virtue of its basis in the Word of God and
its faithful interpretation over the course of time, while the third chapter –
after indicating some of the progress registered by ecumenical dialogue –
specifies some of the disagreements that still exist and invites Christians
to reconsider such issues in the light of the extensive convergence regarding ecclesiology that is claimed throughout the document. In fact, in the
third chapter, the Faith and Order Commission organizes the remaining
disagreements between Christian communities according to a framework
of faith, sacraments, and service/ministry, which roughly corresponds to
seeing the Church as a prophetic, priestly, and royal people of God. The
point seems to be that these are the essential elements which fashion the
Church as "communion" and characterize the Church's activity in mission.
While Christians already share a great deal in terms of faith, worship and
service – one may think, for example, of the profession of the same Nicene
or Apostles' Creed by the vast majority of Christian communities – full
unity is becoming more and more possible as agreement within the context
of legitimate diversity is achieved.

Perhaps a good way to conclude this short essay will be with one of the
closing paragraphs of *The Church: Towards a Common Vision*.

The unity of the body of Christ consists in the gift of *koinonia* or communion
that God graciously bestows upon human beings. There is a growing consensus
that *koinonia*, as communion with the Holy Trinity, is manifested in three interrelated ways: unity in faith, unity in sacramental life, and unity in service (in all
its forms, including ministry and mission). The liturgy, especially the celebration
of the eucharist, serves as a dynamic paradigm for what such *koinonia* looks like
in the present age. In the liturgy, the people of God experience communion with
God and fellowship with Christians of all times and places. They gather with their
presider, proclaim the Good News, confess their faith, pray, teach and learn, offer
praise and thanksgiving, receive the Body and Blood of the Lord, and are sent out
in mission. St John Chrysostom spoke about two altars: one in the Church and the
other among the poor, the suffering and those in distress. Strengthened and nourished by the liturgy, the Church must continue the life-giving mission of Christ in
prophetic and compassionate ministry to the world and in struggle against every
form of injustice and oppression, mistrust and conflict created by human beings
(CTCV, § 67, cf. BS).

The tenth anniversary of the founding of the Protestant Church in the
Netherlands not only deserves congratulations and thanks from Christian
communities throughout the world for the courageous steps that Dutch

Christians have taken in trying to be faithful to the Lord's will for the Church; we may hope that it will also serve as an incentive for all believers to treasure, seek, and preserve the unity of the prophetic, priestly, and royal people of God, which is described in Scripture as Christ's body and as the temple of the Holy Spirit. The more we can together become deeply rooted in our Christian identity, the more the good fruit of unity will be strengthened and grow.

Abbreviations and bibliography

BC: Belhar Confession (1986).

BS: Breklum Statement, by the 9th Forum on Bilateral Dialogues, held in Breklum, Germany in March 2008. In: *The Ecumenical Review* 61(3), October 2009, 343–347; see also http://www.oikoumene.org/en/folder/documents-pdf/breklum-statement.pdf. Accessed May 6, 2014.

CTCV: The Church – Towards a Common Vision (2013). Faith and Order Paper 214. Geneva: WCC Publications 2013. (Versions in English, French, German, Spanish, Korean, Finnish, Italian, and Swedish – with translations in yet other languages to follow – are available at the following internet address: http://www.oikoumene.org/en/resources/documents/wcc-commissions/faith-and-order-commission/i-unity-the-church-and-its-mission/the-church-towards-a-common-vision. Accessed May 6, 2014).

PCN: Protestant Church in the Netherlands.

Calvin, John. 1559. Institutes of the Christian Religion. Two volumes. Edited by John T. McNeill. Translation Ford Lewis Battles 1960. Philadelphia: The Westminster Press – London: SCM.

Uniting and United Churches:
A Living Witness to Organic Unity in the
Twenty-First Century?

An Orthodox perspective

Daniel Buda

Introduction

The role of my paper, as identified by the editors of this volume, was to choose and analyze a few specific theological-ecclesiological issues that run through the first seven contributions of this volume (Parts I and II). I enjoyed total freedom when it came to choosing the theological issues to consider; however, I want to explain why I decided to highlight these themes, rather than other theological-ecclesiological issues, which doubtlessly could pose equal interest to the potential readers of this volume. I will also stress the main questions to which I will try to respond.

Firstly, because the volume is dedicated to the celebration of the fact that it has been ten years since The Protestant Church in the Netherlands was created as the result of a merger between two Dutch Reformed Churches – the Netherlands Reformed Church and the Reformed Churches in the Netherlands – and a Lutheran Church, namely, the Evangelical Lutheran Church in the Kingdom of the Netherlands, it is natural that my study will focus on the *example of organic unity* that has been provided to the ecumenical movement and to other churches by the Dutch churches involved in this merger. As an Orthodox theologian, I have attempted to understand what a merger between three Protestant churches, two Reformed and one Lutheran, might mean for Orthodox ecclesiology. How may the Orthodox understand this merger or similar mergers of this kind, such as the ones that are described in Part II of this volume? Are these mergers able to inspire and encourage inter-orthodox efforts to seek unity, especially in the case of Eastern and Oriental Orthodox Churches? And finally, what do these mergers mean for the ecumenical movement and for the multilateral theological-ecumenical dialogue that has been carried out for many decades, especially by the Commission on Faith and Order? The subsection entitled "The adventure of unions and mergers is going on" has a lot to do with my responsibility for membership matters at the World Council of Churches, and is a brief summary of the unions and mergers in which WCC member churches have been involved during the last few years. It shows that the number of unions and mergers of this kind has increased in recent years.

Secondly, I would like to focus on the role of mission within churches that choose to merge or to form unions. Are uniting and united churches stronger in their sense of mission? Are uniting and united churches a witness by virtue of their own nature and their commitment to organic unity? *Thirdly*, I would like to develop a few reflections concerning the notion of renewal that was associated with uniting and united churches several times in the articles included in Parts I and II of this volume. Are they witnessing to renewal more than other churches? Can they be perceived to be renewal-bringing churches within global Christianity, and if yes, what kind of renewal are they revealing? The attempt to develop reflections like the ones that are encapsulated in the third part of this article is linked to the Faith and Order Conference on renewal that is being planned for 2017 (or 2018). Would it be meaningful to have a session dedicated to "Uniting and United Churches as Renewal-bringing Churches within Global Christianity" at such a conference?

1 Uniting and united churches as living witnesses to organic unity

The first impression that the Orthodox have of the notion of "uniting and uniting churches" is a negative one. It reminds them of the "unions with Rome" involving almost all Orthodox Churches, both Eastern and Oriental, which took place across the centuries during the second millennium of the Christian era. These were unions in which segments of Orthodox Churches agreed – under diverse sorts of pressure – to sign a union with Rome. In English, they are called "uniat churches", in order to differentiate them from the present category of "united and uniting churches", and they are also known as "Greek Catholic churches" in cases where an Eastern Orthodox Church was involved in such a "union." They kept their own traditions, liturgical life, and such, but accepted the primacy of the pope in Rome, along with some other fundamental doctrinal points that are considered to be unique to Catholicism, like *filioque*, purgatory, and the use of azyme, instead of unleavened bread, for the Eucharist. The most well-known agreements on union were signed between Rome and several Orthodox Churches at the Synod of Ferrara-Florence in 1438–9 These served as a model for later unions of this type that were carried out during the Counter-Reformation: agreements of union between Rome and Orthodox Ruthenians and Belarusians living in the Polish-Lithuanian commonwealth, signed at Brest-Litovsk in 1595–6; between Rome and Orthodox Ruthenians from the southern slopes of the Carpathian Mountains, signed at Uzhhorod in 1646; and between Rome and Orthodox Romanians living in Transylvania, signed at Alba Iulia around 1700.

From the ecumenical movement, the Orthodox have learned of the existence of unions and mergers *between* Protestant churches belonging to different traditions. These may be of interest to the Orthodox for at least two reasons. (1) They demonstrate ways that unity has been achieved between Christian churches belonging to the same confessional family (Protestant), but to different traditions (Lutheran, Reformed, and so forth.). (2) They may serve as examples for the dialogue that is going on between the Eastern and Oriental Orthodox traditions.

As described by Professor Koffeman in his article, the history of the process that led to the creation of the PCN contains all of the elements imaginable in such a procedure: a long process that lasted for several decades; long debates regarding church order regulations; difficult discussions about the name of the newly established ecclesial body; issues related to properties and finances; fears expressed by the smaller church involved in the process that its identity would be washed away; questions related to pension benefits for retired ministers, the churches' mortgage obligations with banks, the logo of the newly created church; and, last but not least, the existence of splinter groups that refused to accept the union. The process of the formation of the PCN provides clear evidence that mergers and unions demand great effort and patience. In addition, they involve difficult discussions and a great deal of follow-up which necessarily goes on beyond the accomplishment of the official union. The ratification of a union means the end of a long and difficult process and, at the same time, the beginning of a new journey that could be also long and difficult. The results of such a union are made clear in this assessment of the PCN ten years after its official creation: resources have been consolidated in order to achieve more; the role of the church in a highly secularized country like the Netherlands has been reflected on in new ways in order to better respond to the challenges of our times; the ecumenical spirit has received a new impetus; and the new church is more open to other churches on national, regional, and global levels.

Two elements especially need to be mentioned here because, in my understanding, they are indispensable for any successful and sustainable process of church union or merger. The first one mentioned in the Koffeman article is that "the unification process was, first and foremost, a grass-roots movement." This means that all levels of the church were involved in the process and that everyone had an opportunity to contribute to or to criticize the process – and, in the end, to feel responsible for the decisions made. One of the main characteristics of the "unions with Rome," which were mentioned above, was that they were authorized by the ecclesial and political leadership without proper consultation with the clergy and the laity; thus, they eventually became unpopular and were not accepted by large constituencies of the Church. In the twenty-first century, unions and mergers can be successful only if they involve the entire Body of Christ and only if they respond to intense desires for unity, while fulfilling other immediate needs of the churches involved in the respective unions. The second element that emerges from Koffeman's presentation is the fact that much wisdom, discernment, and sensitivity are demanded from everyone who is involved in such a process of union. Therefore, there are no concrete or generally applicable rules for a successful union between churches. We can learn a lot from similar processes, but it should be clear that each process of ecclesial union is unique. Indeed, "unity is a complicated concept."

Another, rather critical, remark that I need to make here is that to my surprise, theological debate about the creation of the PCN does not seem to have played a central role. Both in the fifth through the seventh centuries and in the twentieth century, the dialogue between the Eastern and Oriental Orthodox Churches was almost exclusively focused on theological and Christological discussions. Of course, this inter-Orthodox dialogue did not progress far enough for constitutional or organizational matters to be considered. However, I would have expected more theological content in the course of the process of creating the PCN, which eventually involved a union between Reformed and Lutheran churches. Yet, the role that the Leuenberg Agreement played in facilitating the unification process of the Dutch churches is clearly highlighted, even if this Agreement was not always mentioned explicitly in the documents that led up to the union. Koffeman mentions the Leuenberg Agreement twelve times in his article. While the Leuenberg Agreement's role in the union that created the PCN is well documented and discussed, I am a bit surprised that the Faith and Order Commission and/or the World Council of Churches are not mentioned directly as playing a part in the unification effort. It is hard to imagine that the work of the Faith and Order Commission in the area of multilateral dialogue and efforts to achieve unity – in which the Dutch churches were deeply involved – did not play any role in their own unification process. However, I was pleased that the role played by the Faith and Order Commission in the formation of The United Reformed Church in the United Kingdom was acknowledged by David M. Thompson in his paper.

I can affirm that for the Orthodox, uniting and united churches are living witnesses to organic unity in the twenty-first century. Orthodoxy – at least as I understand it – is ready to learn from other confessions and to be inspired by what is positive in other churches and religious communities. A careful study of such mergers and unions could be very useful for the Orthodox and inspiring for their own attempts to move toward unity. The unions and mergers that have been achieved between Protestant churches belonging to different traditions are living proof of that fact that reaching unity is not an abstract ideal; it is an occurrence that is taking place today within global Christianity.

Finally, I also promised to say a few words about what these mergers mean for the ecumenical movement and for the multilateral theological-ecumenical dialogue that has been carried out for many decades, especially by the Commission on Faith and Order. I will limit my remarks to an analysis of the place that united and uniting churches are given in recent Faith and Order documents on ecclesiology. In *The Nature and Mission of the Church*, united and uniting churches are recognized as witnessing to "the unity to which God calls us" (NMC, § 2). Their experiences provide precious insight to the ecumenical fellowship (see: Ibid.). They are also mentioned as a particular example of what it means to "grow in fellowship" (NMC, § 3). To my surprise, the notion of "uniting and united churches" does not appear in the last Faith and Order document, which is entitled *The Church; Towards a Common Vision* (CTCV).

2 The adventure of unions and mergers is going on

Part II of this volume contains some case studies related to unions and mergers that have taken place between Protestant churches in Belgium, the United Kingdom, South Africa, and Australia. All of these are examples of mergers and unions that have a history which spans several years. Each of them has its own specificity, which is related to the nature and history of the churches involved; the characteristics of the country in which these churches are located, and other factors. All of these mergers and unions have existed for several years and can finally be evaluated, at least in a preliminary way.

In this subsection, I will simply present the most recent unions and mergers in which member churches of the World Council of Churches have been involved. This list provides strong evidence that unions and mergers between Protestant churches are part of the reality of this branch of Christianity. However, this listing also shows that not only Protestant churches *stricto sensu* are involved in such processes; churches from other traditions are also included.

The Central Committee of the World Council of Churches, which gathered in Kolympari, Greece from August 28 to September 5, 2012, noted the following unions and mergers in which WCC member churches were involved:
– The Estonian Evangelical Lutheran Church Abroad officially merged with the Estonian Evangelical Lutheran Church in November 2010. Both churches were members of the World Council of Churches. Their merger ended a long history of separation caused by Estonia's occupation by the Soviet army and its inclusion in the Soviet Union.
– The Christian Reformed Church in Brazil joined with the Independent Presbyterian Church of Brazil in 2010. Both churches were members of the WCC. The Christian Reformed Church in Brazil was a small church, which was primarily composed of Hungarian migrants. It kept its own autonomy within the Independent Presbyterian church of Brazil;
– Three German regional churches (*Landeskirchen*) – the North Elbian Evangelical Lutheran Church, the Evangelical Lutheran Church of Mecklenburg, and the Pomeranian Evangelical Church – merged on

Pentecost 2012 to form the Evangelical-Lutheran Church in Northern Germany.

– The Reformed Church in Argentina, which was not a member of the WCC, and the Evangelical Church of the River Plate, which is a WCC member church, merged in 2012, keeping the name of the latter church.

The Central Committee of the World Council of Churches, which gathered in Geneva, Switzerland, from July 2 to 8, 2014, noted that the following unions and mergers had occurred since 2012:

– The Reformed Church of France (a WCC member church) and the Evangelical Lutheran Church of France (a WCC member church) entered into union. The name of the new ecclesial body is the United Protestant Church of France.

– The Protestant Church of the Augsburg Confession in Alsace and Loraine (a WCC member church) and the Reformed Protestant Church in Alsace and Loraine (a WCC member church) established a union. The name of the new ecclesial body is the Union of Protestant Churches in Alsace and Loraine.

– The Mission Covenant Church of Sweden (a WCC member church), the Baptist Union of Sweden (which was not a member of the WCC), and the United Methodist Church in Sweden (which was not a member of the WCC) merged in 2013, forming the Uniting Church in Sweden.

The immediate implications of these mergers and unions include the following: (1) In the case of mergers between WCC member churches, the number of WCC member churches is affected, and the goal of reaching unity is furthered in this way. (2) In the case of mergers between WCC member churches and churches that are not members of WCC, the fellowship grows – not in the number of churches, but in its size and witness – and there are more examples of mergers and unions.

Are some Orthodox Churches involved in similar processes of merger and union, or is inter-orthodox dialogue limited to theological discussions between the Eastern and Oriental Orthodox Churches, which, for the time being, have come to a stopping point? The answer to such a question is yes, there are Orthodox Churches involved in such processes. A good example of this is the signing of the Act of Canonical Communion between the Russian Orthodox Church Moscow Patriarchate and the Russian Orthodox Church Outside of Russia in 2007. These two Orthodox Churches were split as a result of historical developments. After the collapse of the tsarist regime in Russia and the implementation of communism, the Russian diaspora and refugees in Western Europe and North America formed the Russian Orthodox Church Outside of Russia. Following the collapse of communism in Russia and Eastern Europe, these churches' reasons for separation no longer existed. Thus, a process of reconciliation and reunification between the two Russian Orthodox Churches began. No doctrinal issues separated the two churches; rather they were divided by different understandings of their common past and negative experiences in relating to each other during the diaspora. The challenge of this reunion involved finding ways to build common structures and to relate to the ecumenical movement.

Why are more and more churches involved in processes of merger and union? Certainly, there are several reasons, but I would like to believe that the first and main reason for such unions and mergers is the call for unity that was addressed to all Christians by Jesus Christ, our God and Savior, when he expressed the hope "that all may be one" (John 17:21). This call for unity is currently being reiterated to Christian churches by global ecumenical organizations like the World Council of Churches and by confessional communities like the Communion of Protestant Churches in Europe, which prepared the Leuenberg Agreement. It is also true that merging enables churches to become stronger in their mission. By uniting their resources, they are able to achieve more. Therefore, I am certain that alongside the call for unity, other burning issues – like limited resources of various kinds, which have been further depleted by the present economic crisis – have encouraged churches to become involved in uniting and/or merging processes. Indeed, there are many paths that bring churches to unity, and some of these are of a non-theological nature.

3 Mission within uniting and united churches

In his paper, Koffeman tells us that the unification process between the three Dutch churches actually "grew of a mission perspective" (see above, 12), It began with an initiative introduced by eighteen ministers from the Netherlands Reformed Church and the Reformed Church in the Netherlands who were working in "mission settings." They were convinced that "by continuing their separate existences, the churches had seriously hampered the credibility of the gospel and the churches' power to witness to Jesus Christ" (see above, 12) On the basis of this account, one can conclude that a concern for mission was at the bottom of the unification process that was undertaken by the Dutch churches. The main reason that the synod of the Evangelical Lutheran Church in the Kingdom of the Netherlands decided to join to the process of forming the Protestant Church in the Netherlands in 1985 was also a missional one. That church "could not do justice to its task of proclaiming the gospel unless it was in collaboration with other denominations."

The simple fact that the new ecclesial body of the PCN had been established encouraged new reflections on its mission and vision. One of the first issues discussed by the synod of the PCN was "the missional aspects of church life." Shortly after the birth of the PCN, a vision-paper entitled *Learning to live out of wonder* was prepared and accepted by the church. According to Dr. Arjan Plaisier, "the most remarkable feature" of the document was "the concept of the church in mission" which became later "a common notion in the church" (see above, 40). For me, it is not surprising to read that the term "mission" was "inflated a bit" (see above, 40), as Dr. Plaisier observes. This is because a newly established church is necessarily more focused on mission than other churches. This conclusion has been confirmed by the mission activity of the PCN during the first years of its existence. One of the main departments of this church is a Mission Department, which has provided intensive assistance at a variety of levels, including within local congregations, in order to encourage them to reflect on the church's mission agenda. The PCN has become the authoritative voice for Protestantism in the Netherlands and understands itself to be a "church for all people, with a mission to the whole of the nation" (see above, 48).

It is also obvious that the creation of a church that is representative of Dutch Protestantism has not created miracles in the Netherlands; the phenomenon of secularization has grown deeper, and church membership has continued to decline. However, it has led to renewed reflection on what mission means for the nature and calling of the church. Thus, Dr. Harm Dane also emphasizes that the simple fact of the initiation of the process of union between the Dutch churches was viewed as "a new starting point, a burst of new energy, and an occasion for reconsidering the church's mission in society" (see above, 50). The idea of a "renewed sense of missionary zeal" was also connected with the history of the United Protestant Church in Belgium (see above, 73).

4 Uniting and united churches as renewal-bringing churches within global Christianity

The word "renewal" appears several times in Parts I and II of this book, where, in most cases, it is associated with the process of re-union and/or merger that is being described. In 1986, the "combi-synod" of the Netherlands Reformed Church and the Reformed Church in the Netherlands signed a Declaration of Intent in which they declared that they were ready to enter into "a process of (re)union and renewal." Two churches from the same tradition (Reformed-Calvinist) divided due to reasons associated with past events were ready to go through a process of "(re)union and renewal." It seems that according to the logic of the authors of the Declaration of Intent, reunion and renewal are so interrelated that no reunion is possible without renewal and that reunion implies renewal as its *conditio sine qua non*. The Declaration of Consensus stressed that "different forms of being church could (and should!) be introduced to a process of (re)union and renewal" (see above, 14).

The Declaration on Unification (which was signed on December 12, 2003) contains a prayer for renewal that was addressed to the Holy Spirit (see above, 32): "We pray for renewal by the Holy Spirit." A few ways to envision renewal are mentioned in terms that express (1) confidence that the Holy Spirit will continue to lead his Church; (2) the desire to proclaim the name of our Lord and to give expression to his love and faithfulness in society; (3) the hope to find each other in the name of the Lord; and (4) a willingness to continue seeking a growing and visible unity for God's Church. In other words, the Declaration on Unification prays for: (1) renewal through the leadership of the Holy Spirit; (2) renewal through a deeper witness to our Lord in their respective society; (3) renewal through a deepening of the fellowship of the newly created church in the name of our Lord; and (4) renewal through a continuing commitment to grow in visible unity. Reading this declaration with its strong commitment to renewal, we may better understand why the first General Secretary of the PCN prayed "come, Holy Spirit, renew your church" in the first sermon delivered in his new capacity.

The notion of "theological renewal" is also used in relationship to the creation of The United Protestant Church of Belgium, and Professor Nico Koopman from South Africa speaks of "uniting for unity, reconciliation, and justice." All three of these dimensions of being united imply "a renewal of the covenant between God and human beings, between human beings themselves, and between human beings and the rest of creation" (see above, 96). Unification thus implies an openness to renewal and transformation, even as we stay focused on the sources of our beliefs and traditions. In this sense, it is not surprising that the word "renewal" appears several times in the Basis of Union of the Uniting Church in Australia. The "coming reconciliation and renewal" (see above, 102) is perceived to be a goal for the whole creation, and commitment to "continuing renewal" within the church is a central aim (see above, 102). In my opinion, renewal should be a continuing process in the sense that we, as Christians and the Church, should always strive to renew our life by continually renewing our relationship to God's revelation through on-going reflection on the way in which the Word of God speaks to us in every age and in every context. Genuine renewal does not mean a simple update because it has a continuing character under the guidance of the Holy Spirit.

Abbreviations and bibliography

CTCV: The Church Towards a Common Vision. Faith and Order Paper 214. Geneva: WCC Publications 2013.
NMC: The Nature and Mission of the Church. Faith and Order Paper 198. Geneva: WCC Publications 1998.
PCN: Protestant Church in the Netherlands.
WCC: World Council of Churches.

Chaillot, Christine, and Alexander Belopopsky (eds.). 1998. Towards unity: the theological dialogue between the Orthodox Church and the Oriental Orthodox Churches, Geneva: Inter-orthodox Dialogue.

Geanakoplos, Deno J. 1955. The Council of Florence (1438 – 39) and the Problem of Union between the Byzantine and Latin Churches. In: Church History 24(1955), 324 – 346; reprinted in: Geanakoplos, Deno J. 1989. Constantinople and the West. Madison: University of Wisconsin Press), 224 – 254.

Gill, Joseph. 1959. The Council of Florence. Cambridge: Cambridge University Press.

Zissis, Theodore. 1990. Uniatism: A Problem in the Dialogue Between the Orthodox and Roman Catholics. In: Greek Orthodox Theological Review, 35(1990), Vol. 1, 21–31.

The Concept of Unity in United and Uniting Churches:
Christological Themes

Randi Jones Walker

In its ten-year history, the Protestant Church in the Netherlands has discovered some tensions arising from the effort to unite churches across confessional lines and lines of differing polities. As the other essays in the collection show, these tensions are, in some ways, distinctively characteristic of united and uniting churches throughout the world. Although these tensions may seem to derive from culture and history, they also stem from ambiguities in the scriptural text and in the different meanings given to the person of Jesus Christ in New Testament literature. There is an age-old division in Christianity between those who conceive of the Christian faith as following Jesus – that is, as a way of life – and those who understand it more as belief in certain propositions about Christ, which then leads to a certain lifestyle. The churches have always held both of these positions, but there are tensions between them. A second common tension lies between those who insist on purity, whether it be of belief or practice, and those who will allow divergences from the doctrinal or moral standards of the church. United and uniting churches have to give up the search for purity; they have to concentrate more on Christianity as a way of life, rather than as an affirmation of specific doctrinal beliefs. Nevertheless, they include individual persons or congregations for whom particular doctrinal confessions are vitally important for their sense of identity, as well as those who believe that purity of confession and practice is necessary in order to please God.

Church and Scripture

The question that all of these united and uniting churches struggle to answer is what is the Church? This question raises others. If Protestants find the answer in Scripture, we have to ask what the Word is. We have more than one answer to this question among our uniting denominations. In the United Church of Christ (UCC) with which I am most familiar, that in the United States, we have a few folks who say that the Word is contained in the words of Scripture taken in their plain meaning. We have many others who say that although divine revelation is in the Word and Scripture expresses this revelation as well as it can in human language, the revelation is not contained in specific words. Rather, the revelation lies in the meaning of those words, and, as the text is read in communion with the Holy Spirit, generation by generation, "yet more light and truth will break forth from the Word" – to use a phrase coming from the Puritan Congregational tradition, and particularly from John Robinson, one of the Puritan pastors in England in the seventeenth century. The authority to say what the Word is for any given time lies in the congregation itself, in the persons who are called to teach and preach, and in the living tradition of the Church throughout history, but not in any one of these alone.

The nature of the Church is proclaimed In Scripture, but in more than one way. Certainly, the Church is the Body of Christ. The Church is a community called out of the world by God, an *ecclesia*. In addition, the Church shares with Judaism the sense of being in a community created by a covenant. As the people of Israel were and are constituted by a covenant with God, so too, the Church is invited into a covenant established by God. If the Church is the Body of Christ or if Christ is the head of the Church, then we may also ask who Christ is. A particular confession about the nature of Christ often entails a particular stance toward the tensions presented above. If a person understands Christ to be the judge of the living and the dead, purity of thought and life will be critically important, whereas if a person understands Christ to be the healer and savior of souls, an openness to the presence of those who are not perfect or who have diverse views and ways of being Christian is entailed. If the Church is somehow associated with the kingdom of God and is a community called out by God, does the Church already live in the kingdom of God, and if so, how?

Unity and Social Gospel

Many united and uniting churches first began conversations leading toward union in the midst of the early ecumenical movement in the twentieth century. The people in those conversations participated in the Christian Life and Work Movement, in the Student Christian Movement, or in other manifestations of the ecumenical ferment of those years. They were deeply affected by the Social Gospel, the effort to create society in the shape of the kingdom of God. If they felt some apocalyptic urgency in this task, they described it as an urgency to make the world fit for the return of Christ. They were evangelists, not only for the conversion of individuals to the faith, but also for the conversion of society and its structures. In the thought of the Social Gospel, the church was the body charged with the proclamation of the gospel – a view close to that of the Lutheran partner in the Protestant Church in the Netherlands (see above, 16) –, but for the kingdom of God to be manifested on earth, it was necessary to form a public conscience geared toward social and economic justice and peace. This idea of the reign of Christ in the kingdom of God has contributed to the urgency of these unification efforts among churches. Several of the essays point out connections and tensions that exist among their constituent traditions with regard to issues of social justice and human service. The ecclesiology of several of the united and uniting churches emphasizes the *missio Dei* or the Church as the servant of Christ in the service of humanity. In many ways, it is easier to see the unity of the Church in this servant role than it is to recognize it in the attempts at doctrinal clarity that ironically have made unity so difficult.

United and uniting churches most often cite Jesus' high priestly prayer in the Gospel of John as being the compelling scriptural reason for their union efforts. "May they all be one as You and I are one" is an entreaty that makes unity necessary. If we ignore the call to unity, if we are satisfied that it is possible to love one another without living in unity, we have not really learned to love. Unity is possible in narrow ways. There is a kind of Reformed unity, Lutheran unity, or Methodist unity; at least there is unity within the smaller branches of these world communions. Local congregations have a kind of persistent unity. However, these unities are fragile. All it takes to create tension, quarreling, and a division is someone who believes that someone else in the community has compromised the purity of the faith in some way. United and uniting churches have all created further divisions as a consequence of their efforts to unite. All of the authors of the essays in this collection struggle with the tensions of unity amid clear diversities.

Unity and the Aristotelian We

Dr. Dane uses Bonhoeffer's typologies of "We" to discuss aspects of the experience of the Protestant Church of The Netherlands (see above, 52ff.). These typologies apply to all of us in united and uniting churches, and they may be useful in sorting out the diverse theological versions of We in the New Testament. One aspect of our tensions and further divisions lies in our different understandings of what we mean by We.

The Aristotelian We, the polis, operates as a communal identity marker; it is a We located in place and time and the We to which one is born, belongs, and dies. This We is a container of identity, a system of relationships that holds us in place in society. It is like the Body of Christ. The Body of Christ holds us in a container of identity, as a part indispensable to the other parts. We are born into it, and we recognize our belonging through our baptism and confirmation. We live in and through the Body as we carry out our calling as disciples. When we die, the church holds us, mourns us, and recognizes us as part of the great cloud of witnesses that still upholds the church. This is an organic We. Dane points out that the Aristotelian We can become stifling and dictatorial. In contrast, the body as an organic system does not function as a dictatorship. Only with disease, injury, or death does one part of the body overstep its place in the whole. Yet, the loss of one part can create hardship for the rest of the body. It is a whole like the polis.

With the splintering of Protestantism over the last four centuries, we have created a large number of hands, feet, eyes, and other parts, each insisting that this part of the body is the body and that the others are untrue to the body because they are not hands, feet, or eyes. With courage, faith, martyrdom, and the effort of hard human work, each of these parts has recreated a kind of body from a single part. Each of these parts has satisfied many thousands of people, but the longing to be part of the whole Body has never left them. Those in whom the longing to be part of the whole Body has grown the strongest have sought reunion with some of the other parts. The Body of Christ is still one; the parts are becoming more aware and are drawing themselves back together. The Vine is a similar metaphor found in the New Testament. The united and uniting churches are grafting themselves together or recognizing that they are part of the same Vine, even if – as branches – they grew so far from the main stem that they forgot that we are connected to the same roots. We find our unity in Christ who has held it for us all along.

Unity and the Cartesian We

Dane's description of Bonhoeffer's Cartesian We invites reflection on the factor of congregationalism within our traditions. Understanding the many as being united in their penchant for sharing a common regard for freedom, equality, and holding certain rights is a way of thinking about unity that is very different from one which is associated with the Body of Christ. The tensions within our traditions regarding the freedom of the congregation are significant. In the United Church of Christ in the U.S.A., we have enshrined the autonomy of the local congregation in our constitution and bylaws. This high regard for the local congregation reflects the picture of the earliest churches that is found in the New Testament. They seem to be a collection of locally organized churches, held together only loosely by the visits of traveling apostles like Paul; by the circulation of letters containing news, advice, and encouragement; and, after a time, by a shared group of texts which they regarded as sacred. The organization of extended groups of congregations into dioceses governed by a bishop developed later, as the church settled itself into the Roman political order. In the UCC, one of the uniting churches voted *congregation by congregation* to join the union; these were the Congregational Christian Churches. The other uniting church, the Evangelical and Reformed Church, voted *as a synod* to join; whether or not they individually agreed with the decision, all of the congregations became part of the united church.

Within the UCC, there are differing understandings of the main location of the Body of Christ and the degree to which the church is the Body of Christ when it meets in its General Synod. This is a Christological question that we have not yet wrestled with and solved. It comes to the surface entangled with postmodern political divisions and social justice commitments. It is a spiritual problem, as well as a theological one, because the experience of the sacrament of the Lord's Supper (the Eucharist) is not yet central to meetings of the church that take place beyond the local congregational setting. By this, I mean that we do not constitute ourselves as church,

meeting Christ at the table before we begin to do business; rather, we celebrate the sacrament later in the meeting after the business is completed.
We do not understand ourselves as a eucharistic community in our wider
church meetings. We understand ourselves congregationally, and in this
respect, the Cartesian We describes the way we understand ourselves as a
communion of congregations quite well. The achievement of this Cartesian
unity is no mean accomplishment, but it is not the same thing as recognizing ourselves to be the Body of Christ.

Unity and the Stoic We

As Dane described Bonhoeffer's Stoic We, the Sermon on the Mount from
Matthew's Gospel came to mind. Christologically conceived, the Stoic We
may be something that derives from the Body of Christ or the Vine. The
We that is formed in empathy with each other lies close to the heart of those
who were active in many of these unification efforts because of their social
justice commitments and vision of a stronger church that would be better
able to serve the world. In the Sermon on the Mount, Matthew presents
Jesus preaching on the way to live life in its fullness. Nothing is overtly
expressed about unity. However, there are many teachings about how to
treat other people as human beings and how to live life as part of humanity,
rather than as a solitary individual who must look out for herself. There is
nothing here about competition, efficiency, or having things our way. The
unity that results from the application of the Sermon on the Mount is a
unity of reconciliation and service.

This is the unity that is lived out in the Uniting Reformed Church in
Southern Africa. There, as in many of our united and uniting churches,
the presence of cultural, ethnic, and racial diversity has created persistent
kinds of division that are not related to the doctrinal differences over which
we have struggled for so long. This kind of division usually presents itself in terms of differences in class and privilege. We enjoy a vision of a
multiracial, multicultural church and imagine congregations of all nations,
tongues, and races. In the United Church of Christ in the U.S.A., we made
a pronouncement about that ideal. Some put pressure on our congregations that represent particular minority ethnic or racial backgrounds to be
less ethnic or even, in a couple of cases with which I am familiar, to dis-
band and join white churches. Rarely do European Americans join Native
American, Japanese, Latino, or Black congregations in the UCC. If a few

families of other races or cultures join a white congregation, they claim that they are multiracial or multicultural. We still do things in the manner of our European American church cultures. Racism remains a persistent threat to our unity. The Sermon on the Mount and a Stoic conception of We could help return us to a sense of the Body of Christ in our practice of the Christian faith. This would be a unity of disciplined practice, rather than a unity of theological concepts. In addition, it would be a spiritual unity born of walking in the way of Christ. The Uniting Church in Australia calls itself a pilgrim church. We are all going toward unity in Christ, but are not there yet. Nevertheless, something of that unity can realize itself in us in the journey itself, as we carry burdens with each other, listen closely, and stand up for each other's dignity.

Unity and the Epicurean We

Dane suggests that the Epicurean We is a fragile We. This We can disintegrate into fragmented individualism. However, this We can love neighbor as self, precisely because this We can love self. The Epicurean We is foreign to the Protestant tradition with its roots not only in Scripture, but also in Augustinian theology. Augustine had a dim view of the human ability to find the ability to love others in self-love. Luther probably understood that in order to love others, we need to love ourselves in a healthy way. In his life story, he moved from a period of self-destructive anxiety about his acceptability to God to an understanding of grace. Calvin said less about himself, so we do not know whether he understood self-love in a similar way. Calvin's writings were more severe. His followers cautioned people to be careful not to claim an experience of God's grace too easily. During the Pietist movements of the seventeenth and eighteenth centuries, some of the resultant groups – particularly those of an Armenian Methodist variety – became perfectionists. Holiness and sanctification required following the Word of God perfectly. This perfectionism lent itself well to modern organized industrial production. There is little place for grace in the modern economy. Love of self is both everywhere and hard to find. Consumer culture fosters self-indulgence, and advertising preaches about the perfection of physical features, the gratification of desire, and a life of happiness. In the Epicurean sense, we support others' abilities to indulge themselves by spending money to indulge ourselves. The church could ask if this is real self-love. Self-love moves us to health, to acceptance of ourselves, to courage to act out of respect for our convictions, and to the awareness of others that is possible because we understand ourselves.

Conclusion

With this, we circle back to the Body of Christ. Those who are engrafted into the Vine or are part of the Body participate in the ebb and flow of life keenly aware of having a place, of being held together in a container of identity, and of participating in a kind of solidarity. United and uniting churches such as the Protestant Church in the Netherlands began from traditions that rooted themselves in a unity based on shared doctrinal standards and ways of organizing themselves as church. Yet, the united and uniting church must seek its unity in a different place. Christological unity grounded in the spiritual experience of the Body of Christ and the sacramental presence of Christ at the table at all gatherings of the church lays a foundation for unity. Along with this, a disciplined discipleship, being on the way together with Christ, and following the way of reconciliation and justice will not put us in the kingdom of God all the time, but will give us glimpses and tastes of that kingdom along the way. Having confidence and faith in God's love for each person and every congregation so that love for others may flourish will provide the unity needed amid the ambiguities and tensions that distinguish our diverse creeds, our diverse people, and our relationship to societies that are facing rapid social change. If they seek a simple understanding of We, our united and uniting churches may miss the rich Christological texture that characterizes the gathered people called to be the church.

Abbreviations

UCC: United Church of Christ.

List of Authors

Prof. Hugh Robert Boudin (1926) is Hon. Rector of the Faculté Universitaire de Théologie Protestante de Bruxelles – Universitaire Faculteit voor Protestantse Godgeleerdheid te Brussel, Belgium, and Professor at the Université Libre de Bruxelles and the Faculté de Théologie Protestante de Butare, Rwanda. He is an ordained minister of the United Protestant Church of Belgium. Previously National Boy's Work secretary of the Y.M.C.A. of Belgium. Warden of the International Centre Castle Mainau (Lake of Constance). Pastor of the Eglise Wallonne de Cantorbéry. He published *La Croix et la Bannière. Les Protestants et les Anglicans en Belgique face à l'Occupation 1940–1944* and *Dictionnaire historique du protestantisme et de l'anglicanisme en Belgique depuis le XVIme siècle jusqu'à nos jours* (forthcoming).

As. Prof. Daniel Buda (1977) is staff member of the Faith and Order Commission of the World Council of Churches, As. Professor for Church History at the Orthodox Theological Faculty "Andrei Saguna" of Lucian Blaga University, Sibiu, Romania, and Research Fellow at the University of Pretoria (South Africa). He is Archpriest of the Romanian Orthodox Church since 2008 and served as Local Organiser of the Third European Ecumenical Assembly, Sibiu 2007, and as Program Executive for Church and Ecumenical Relations in the WCC between 2009 and 2013. He published *The Orthodox Churches and the Ecumenical Movement at the Beginning of the 21st Century* (in Romanian; Sibiu: Astra Museum Publishing, 2014).

Dr. Harm G. Dane (1949) is a staff member, with particular responsibility for theological and sociological questions, at the main office of the Protestant Church in the Netherlands, in Utrecht. He published *Verlichting en vergeving: over kerkelijk vormingswerk* (Zoetermeer: Boekencentrum, 1995).

Prof. Andrew Dutney (1958) is the President of the Uniting Church in Australia for the triennium 2012–2015. He is Professor of Theology at Flinders University. Prior to being installed as UCA President he was the Principal of Uniting College for Leadership & Theology, within the Adelaide College of Divinity. He is a leading authority on the history and theology of the UCA, his books on the subject including *Manifest for Renewal: The Shaping of a New Church* (Melbourne: Uniting Church Press, 1986), *Where Did the Joy Come From? Rediscovering the Basis of Union* (Melbourne: Uniting Church Press, 2001) and *A Genuinely Educated Ministry: Three Studies on Theological Education in the Uniting Church in Australia* (Adelaide: MediaCom Education Inc, 2007 and 2011).

Prof. William Henn, OFM Cap., (1950) is Professor of Ecclesiology at the Pontifical Gregorian University in Rome. He is a priest of the Roman Catholic Church. On behalf of the Pontifical Council for Promoting Christian Unity, he shares in a number of dialogue groups, including the WCC Faith & Order Commission and the joint groups with the Mennonite and the Lutheran churches, and with the Reformed churches. He published *Church: The People of God* (London: Burns & Oates / New York: Continuum, 2004).

Prof. Leo J. Koffeman (1948) is Professor of Church Polity and Ecumenism at the Protestant Theological University (location Amsterdam) in the Netherlands, and an Extraordinary Professor at the University of Stellenbosch and the University of Pretoria (South Africa).
He is an ordained minister of the Protestant Church in the Netherlands, and he has been serving as an ecumenical officer of his church for about 25 years. He is a member of the Faith and Order Commission. He published *In Order to Serve: An Ecumenical Introduction to Church Polity* (Zürich: LIT-Verlag, 2014).

Prof. Nico N. Koopman (1961) is Professor of Systematic Theology and currently Dean of the Faculty of Theology at the University of Stellenbosch (South Africa). Since 2002 he also serves as Director of the Beyers Naudé Centre for Public Theology. He is an ordained minister of the Uniting Reformed Church in Southern Africa. Together with Robert Vosloo he published *Die ligtheid van die lig. Morele oriëntasie in 'n postmoderne tyd* (Lux Verbi, 2002), that won the prestigious Andrew Prize for Theological

Literature (2003). One of his latest publications is a monograph titled *Cries for a humane life. Reflections on the Lord's prayer* (Wellington: Bible Media, 2014).

Dr. Arjan Plaisier (1956) is the General Secretary of the Protestant Church in the Netherlands. He is an ordained minister of his church. From 1986 till 1992 he taught at the Theological Seminary at Ujung Pandang (now Makassar) in Indonesia. He published *Overvloed en overgave: een caleidoscopisch geloofsboek* (Zoetermeer: Boekencentrum, 2013).

Prof. David M. Thompson (1942) is Emeritus Professor of Modern Church History at the University of Cambridge (United Kingdom). He was formerly also the Director of the Centre for Advanced Religious and Theological Studies from 1995 until his retirement in 2009. In addition he was a Fellow of Fitzwilliam College Cambridge (1965–2009) and is now a Life Fellow. He is an ordained minister of the United Reformed Church, and the author of *Cambridge Theology in the Nineteenth Century: Enquiry, Controversy and Truth* (Basingstoke: Ashgate, 2008).

Prof. Randi Walker (1952) is Professor of Church History and Director of the Doctor of Ministry Program at the Pacific School of Religion in Berkeley, CA, USA. She is an ordained minister in the United Church of Christ in the United States and has served on the UCC Council for Ecumenism and is currently a UCC Representative to the U.S. Reformed/Roman Catholic dialogue on Ecclesiology. She is the author of *The Evolution of a UCC Style: Essays in the History and Culture of the United Church of Christ* (Cleveland, OH: United Church Press, 2005) and *Religion and the Public Conscience: Ecumenical Civil Rights Work in Seattle 1940–1960* (Winchester, UK: Circle Books, 2013).

Church Polity and Ecumenism

Global Perspectives

edited by Prof. Dr. Leo J. Koffeman (Amsterdam), Prof. Dr. Allan J. Janssen (New Brunswick/USA), Prof. Dr. Johannes Smit (Potchefstroom/South Africa and Dr. C. Leon van den Broeke (Amsterdam)

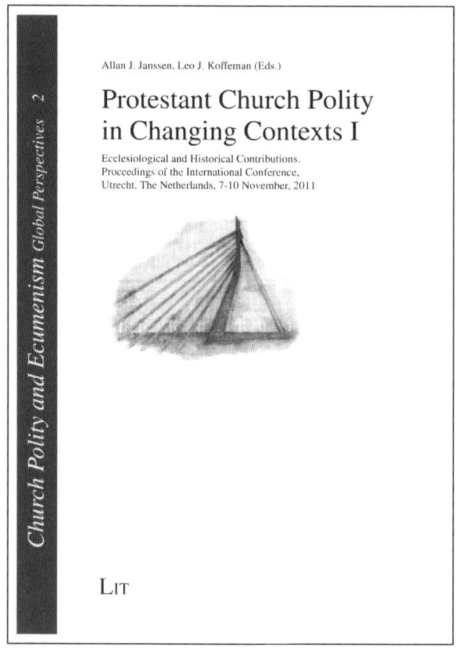

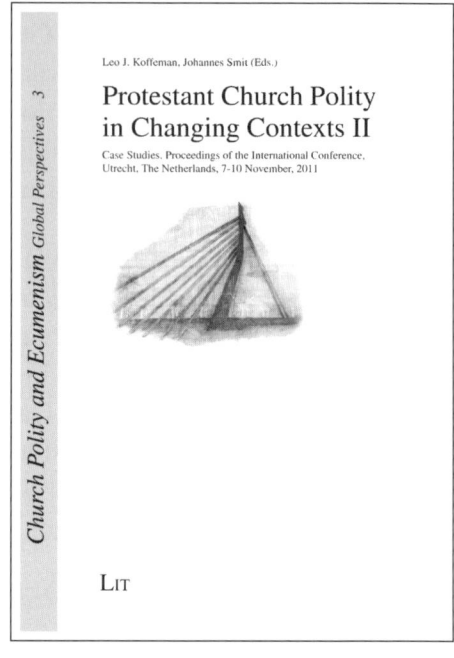

Allan J. Janssen; Leo Koffeman (Eds.)
Protestant Church Polity in Changing Contexts I
Ecclesiological and Historical Contributions. Proceedings of the International Conference, Utrecht, The Netherlands, 7 – 10 November, 2011
Church polity as a theological discipline has become increasingly aware of the challenge of contextuality, due to tendencies like secularization in the global North and a renewed awareness of inherited cultural and religious traditions in the global South. The ecumenical movement offers a particular framework for reflection on such developments.
This first conference volume contains studies in the fields of ecclesiology, church history, missiology, inter-cultural theology and practical theology. A second volume presents a number of case studies.
Bd. 2, 2014, 216 S., 29,90 €, br., ISBN 978-3-643-90310-5

Leo J. Koffeman; Johannes Smit (Eds.)
Protestant Church Polity in Changing Contexts II
Case Studies. Proceedings of the International Conference, Utrecht, The Netherlands, 7 – 10 November, 2011
Church polity as a theological discipline has become increasingly aware of the challenge of contextuality, due to secularization in the global North and a renewed awareness of inherited cultural and religious traditions in the global South. The ecumenical movement offers a particular framework for reflection on such developments.
This second conference volume presents thirteen case studies, from five continents, and covering church polity issues from perspectives like practical theology, civil law, and missiology. Another volume presents a number of ecclesiological and historical reflections.
Bd. 3, 2014, 208 S., 29,90 €, br., ISBN 978-3-643-90311-2

LIT Verlag Berlin – Münster – Wien – Zürich – London

Auslieferung Deutschland / Österreich / Schweiz: siehe Impressumsseite